POWER OF FOUR

WIND AND WATER

SEVEN BORUP

Publishing Services provided by Paper Raven Books
Printed in the United States of America
First Printing, 2021

Paperback ISBN= 978-1-7363042-2-8
Hardback ISBN= 978-1-7363042-3-5

CHAPTER ONE

Water strutted confidently into the large ceremonial room and sat facing the raised section of the floor, his bearing tall and proud. His litter brother Nettle padded into the room, followed closely by Blizzard. Water basked in the soft glow of the moonlight, knowing how it turned his blue-gray fur to a mesmerizing silver. This was the most important moment of his life, and he was not nervous, yet he couldn't summon any excitement.

Nettle, on the other hand, was bunched into himself, hunched over and glancing about anxiously. He appeared to shiver slightly.

"What is wrong with you?" Water whispered sharply through the side of his mouth.

"Nothing. Just face forward," Nettle shot back.

Deerface suddenly emerged through the entryway and sat down on the dais calmly, his white paws tucked together in front of him. One at a time, the other three leaders filed in and sat down on the dais, all lined up perfectly. Water felt it strange to think that Deerface was his brother, when he had stepped in as a fatherly figure, and acted as one all of Water's life so far.

"Welcome," Deerface boomed, his brown eyes gleaming with pride. "It is my honor to begin this ceremony. Now, without further ado, Water, come here, please."

Water stepped forward and met Deerface's eyes boldly, forcing himself to not break their strong gaze. "Water, though you are still very young, I feel that you have already come far in your life. You have the strength of our father but the purity and heart of a colony rabbit. You will find many opportunities for greatness and glory, and one day you may even be sitting up here as a leader, gazing down at the next generation as I do now. I am immensely proud of you. May you live your life in a way that you can share that pride in yourself, and may you fully receive our blessing."

Water stood as still as he could as all four leaders moved forward and dipped their heads to him. He towered above both Stewie and Runt.

He stepped back once more as Nettle took his place. He barely paid attention, letting his mind wander.

Every rabbit he'd ever met had told him how great he was going to be, how strong and courageous. Rabbits of his colony would even drop by the den as they went about their business just to get a look at him, remarking on his already broad, powerful shoulders, his huge paws and silky fur. Of course, Water liked the praise, but he just felt so… incomplete. He felt *empty*.

He felt Nettle's coat brush against his own as they stood next to one another once more.

"Nettle, you will be a Messenger, with Scale training you to deliver messages. Water, you will serve as a Patroller, and will be taught how to fight by Light," Runt announced, his voice sounding frail compared to Deerface's. "Your training starts tomorrow morning, so don't be late."

CHAPTER TWO

A figure dawned on top of the split stone that overshadowed the entire clearing. Wind felt cold as the other exiles shifted away from him and his leader's pale green gaze sought him out. What job could he possibly wish for among this pack of criminals?

"*Wind*." She drew his name sharply over her tongue. She looked thoughtful. "You have come of age to be recognized as one of us."

"Who'll be my instructor?" he asked boldly.

Silver's eyes narrowed, and she edged forward. "You poor little fellow, so very *confused*." She raked her claws over her rocky perch, and he flinched. "We will all teach you at some point or another. From me, you can learn your *place*." Silver leapt down gracefully and stalked up to him, stopping when her face was just inches from his own. Her eyes bored into his, sinking the claws of her hate into his very heart. He gasped.

"Patch. Come here." She summoned a black-and-white rabbit that was only a little older than him. "Patch here was a runt of his litter, so his mother abandoned him at our border. You will fight him to show all of us if combat comes as naturally to you as it did to Billy. Are you afraid?"

"I am not," he spat, puffing out his chest.

"Good." She now had to look up at him. "Now prove it." She stepped back and sat down.

Patch glared up at Wind, silently evaluating him. He hesitated.

"I said *fight!*" Silver screeched.

Wind immediately flew at Patch, who reared up to attempt to catch him. He staggered backward under Wind's bulk, and Wind grabbed for his scruff. He found it and hauled Patch to the side, but his opponent let himself be dragged. Why wasn't he fighting back?

"Congratulations, Wind. You have won."

"What? But he didn't say he gave in." Wind yanked again.

"If the dead could talk, he would've. It looks as if you crushed his spine when you landed on him," Silver observed, appearing unmoved.

Wind fought the urge to leap back in horror, not wanting to appear weakened by the sight of death so soon after his victory. Instead, he dropped Patch and sniffed. "Pity, I thought you'd give me a challenge."

"You want a challenge, *kit?*" Her eyes glinted. "Crimson! Show this kit a challenge, please. Do not kill him, but fight him. Is that clear?"

A reddish-brown male rabbit with brown eyes growled low in his throat as he came to stand beside his leader. He was her second-in-command, condemned for numerous accounts of murder and treason from back when Billy had still ruled. "It is."

Wind took a good look at his new challenger. Even though he was not fully grown, they were equal in size. But this rabbit didn't look particularly smart, and maybe he wasn't, since he had ended up here. He appeared to have a fresh cut on his hip, most likely from a scuffle. Wind felt relieved. *He's already weakened. I might have a chance here.*

With a roar, Crimson charged him like an unworldly creature. Wind dodged. Crimson whirled around, and Wind faced him head-on. *Okay, he's slower than me,* he noted. *Good to know.*

When Crimson charged again, Wind used his momentum to flip neatly over his back and land behind him. He sliced at Crimson's fresh wound and it opened. Crimson screeched and crumpled to the ground as blood pumped from the wound. He would not get up again.

"Incredible," Silver whispered. "You, Wind, have barely started training and have already killed two rabbits, including my second-in-command. Was it difficult?"

He shrugged, uncomfortable. "No, not really."

"I'm not talking about simply fighting them. I'm talking about *killing* them. Was that hard for you to do? Do you regret it?" she pried.

He thought for a moment, then looked back at her. "I guess not. I mean, they *were* trying to hurt me."

"Did you *enjoy* the kill?" she asked, tipping her head to one side. The other rabbits in the clearing shifted about uneasily as they awaited his answer. Very few actually killed for entertainment. Most had done it because they felt they had to, whether it was to defend themselves or a loved one.

What should he say? Maybe answering yes would make them all fear him, and impress even the most dangerous exiles, even Silver herself. Saying no would make him look weak in front of them, and that was suicidal.

Keeping his gaze level with hers with emotionless eyes, he answered, "I did. It felt right."

"That's because it *is* right, Wind," she said authoritatively. "It makes us stronger and smarter than those mangy colony rabbits." She raised her voice so as to be heard by all. "We need more rabbits like Wind! Unafraid to do what needs to be done, detached from the sentimentality that is our greatest weakness! We must dispose of this useless feeling!"

He stood taller, proud to have been singled out.

"Wind, I want to train you myself," Silver told him quietly. "You must be given the best of training, and then what a credit you'll be to us! Do you understand? I want you to make me a promise."

"Anything." He nodded excitedly.

"I want you to promise me that if I train you, you will stand by me as my most loyal subject, *no matter what*."

"I promise!" he declared, eyes wide.

"Good." She closed her eyes briefly, then retreated to her den without another word.

The other exiles pressed around him, offering their congratulations. Wind found it odd. Crimson had been their friend and their ally, and Wind's claws were stained red with his blood. Were they trying to get on good terms with him to avoid ending up like Crimson?

Wind acknowledged their congratulations with a nod, and they scampered off. As soon as he was alone, Darkside stalked up and signaled him to follow him to a quieter, shady place.

"What do you think you're *doing?* You said you'd be loyal to me, you *swore* it! Why let Silver ruin that for us? We could still rule together, as brothers!" Darkside snarled, brown eyes boring into Wind.

"No, I made that promise when I was barely two weeks old. I don't make kit promises anymore. That's the best part about living in a camp of liars and murderers: words don't matter! This is my best option."

"And what of me? Have you considered where *I* fit into all of this?" Darkside spat.

"You *don't*, Darkside. I don't need you anymore, so beat it. You've got nothing on me."

Darkside's eyes blazed with rage.

"You listen here, you colony filth! Your sorry pelt wouldn't be here without me. I was the one to bring you here, to negotiate with Silver. You *owe* me."

"I owe you nothing. That was *your* mistake, your downfall to bring me here. And in this place, kinship counts for nothing."

Darkside gritted his teeth, then whirled around and stormed off. Wind watched him go in silence.

He thinks I'll just give in to sentimentality for a wretch like him? No way! He's trying to trick me since he has no chance with fighting me. He wants to make me weak and then take me out.

Shoulders hunched, he lounged at the edge of camp. No rabbit dared to approach him, to disturb him. In just a few short moments, all of their lives had changed drastically. They now had a sense of his strength, and they knew that he was in charge.

He let out a long breath, raised his head, and looked around. As if he'd been waiting for a cue, Slicer approached Wind cautiously. "Silver wants a word with you, beside her den."

"Fine." He arose and left without question.

Silver was grooming her velvety ears in the pool of sunlight beside the split rock. "Wind," she said evenly as he approached, "let's train while there's still light to see by. But before we begin, I want to remind you of your promise, that you will try to not injure me, so that I may teach you."

"Of course," he said with a small nod.

"Then we can train here." She motioned toward the shade. "It is your job to help me enforce my will and power. I will only teach you the moves that I have kept secret, so you'll have the upper-paw over them in combat. Are you ready?"

"Always." He nodded swiftly.

She narrowed her eyes to slits before leaping up high, making for his shoulders. He reared up in defense, but just before her jump was completed, she dove downward into a somersault, her back feet striking outwards, into his stomach. He was kicked backward viciously, winded, as a bush caught him. Wind lurched forwards, gasping for breath.

Silver sat complacently across the training space, as if the short scuffle hadn't cost her an ounce of energy. "Would you like to try again?" her voice dripped with mockery, while she cocked her head slyly.

"Again." He regained his breath, steadied himself, and this time started the training bout. Wind decided that he would duck low this time and try to knock her feet out from under her. That would leave her stomach exposed to another attack.

He crept forward as she waited, her expression unreadable. He shot forward, still keeping close to the ground, but she sidestepped him and hooked her claws into his side to flip him over. He landed flat on his back, his belly exposed and vulnerable.

He flailed briefly as she planted a paw on his chest and hissed in his face. "Not fast enough! You could have beaten me if you had faked the charge and swerved to the side to face me head on."

He squirmed out from under her paw and stood up. "I didn't expect you to move."

"Next time, you will. And your eyes betrayed where you were going to attack first." She shoved him away. "Now try it again. But this time, keep your options of movement open, not your vulnerabilities."

"Understood," Wind answered stoutly.

He pinned his eyes on her paws again, secretly planning to attack from above. He darted forward and, at the last second, reared up. But Silver tucked in her paws, ducked her head, and rolled between his widely planted legs. But when she popped up behind him, he was ready. He swiveled around fluidly, batted her away, and pounced again. She gritted her teeth in a snarl, recovered before he finished the attack, and pushed off of the ground. She twisted in the air and vaulted over his back, landing neatly on her paws, ready for the next attack. They were right back where they had started.

"Pretend that a rabbit is trying to attack low. There are usually two things you can do in such a quick, immediate attack: you can sidestep and counter, as you saw me do earlier, or you can leap right above their head, keeping your hind legs up higher than your head, and use your forelegs to shove their shoulders downward. Watch what I do, then copy it."

Silver jumped up, then dove downward on the same spot, her front paws hitting the ground forcefully. He flinched at the thought of what that could do to a rabbit's neck or spine.

Silver faced him again, holding his gaze seriously. "We won't practice that move together because it is often lethal, but I'm sure you'll get the opportunity to try it out for yourself when one of these idiots screws up. That's all we can do for today. And make sure your den is separate from the others'. They're a little too fond of playing dirty tricks." Without saying anything else, Silver abruptly turned and disappeared into her small cave, the darkness swallowing her gleaming silver pelt. All was silent.

Wind turned away with a sigh of exhaustion, eyes prodding the dim, overgrown edges of the hard-packed little grove. A dense bramble thicket was partially hidden among large patches of bracken. He stumbled toward it and found a narrow gap in one side that faced away from the clearing. He thrust his head and shoulders into the gap, widening it into a makeshift entrance until he could fit inside of the mostly hollow interior of the bush. Wind used his shoulders to shore up the walls as best he could in the gloom, brushed aside debris, and tucked the prickly stray tendrils into the roof and walls.

He returned outside to gather as many leaves as he could, jamming them into his jaws and carrying them into the den. After several trips, he had gathered enough to shape a semi-comfortable nest, which he settled down in. Wind rested his head on his paws and gazed out the entrance. Now that he was alone, not busy training, fighting, or talking with other rabbits, a feeling of loneliness overcame him. He felt hollow and heavy at the same time, like the floor of the den was sucking his paws down into it.

It would be so nice to have a true, loyal comrade to talk to and to count on, a rabbit who would always support me, and never betray me… Wind reflected wistfully as he drifted off into sleep.

CHAPTER THREE

Water emerged into the harsh sunlight and blinked rapidly to clear his vision. Light looked more nervous than he felt. Water would be his first ever student.

"Y-Your first training session will be with a group. We'll just wait a little bit longer for them," Light said edgily, shifting his feet as he studied them.

Water occasionally flexed his paws in impatience. He knew that he must impress his fellow trainees and their instructors. It was vital for him to be able to fit in with the group.

A half-grown, dusky red male rabbit emerged from the entrance of the tunnel, pelt ruffled and still yawning, while another dark gray male followed on his heels, along with a brownish-red and white female. They butted shoulders and scuffled playfully, while their instructors, much more composed, cautiously followed on their heels.

"These are Cedar, Root, and Boulder. Their instructors are Fern and Bramble. They are your denmates. Where's Root's instructor?" Light peered over their shoulders, back at the tunnel.

"Sick, I'm afraid. He stayed in," Fern answered sullenly. "So I'll be leading the session for today."

"Rightly so," Bramble muttered. "Shall we get started with a bout of Pass and Capture?"

"We haven't enough rabbits here for that, I'm afraid. One-on-one would do," Fern suggested.

"But this is Water's first day! You can't expect him to be able to keep up with the older students!" Light objected.

"Why not? Do you doubt me?" Water accused.

"Of course not, but let's just take things slow at first." Light glared at him, a warning to back down and obey.

Water gritted his teeth, irritation welling up inside of him.

"If he wants to do it, then I say let him," Fern cut in sharply.

"He's *my* student!"

"And *I'm* the one leading this session, or have you forgotten so quickly?" Fern retorted, eyes smoldering with indignation.

"Fine, but his injuries are on you," Light growled.

"At last!" Boulder exclaimed. "Can we start now?"

"Yes. You and I will spar, while Cedar and Water will go head-to-head," Fern instructed.

"And remember to fight fair. No biting or clawing. We aren't exiles, for rabbit's sake!" Bramble added hastily, glancing at Cedar, who huffed indignantly in response.

Without comment, Water trotted over to take his place across from Cedar.

"Whoa, slow down! This is just a training session, not a raid!" Cedar joked.

"Whatever. Let's just get on with it," he muttered.

Cedar's face hardened. "If you want to have attitude, then fine. But it doesn't help. Never has."

"I don't need help." Water leapt at Cedar with a toothy, violent snarl. Surprised, Cedar fell back, and Water missed by a hair. He whipped around and struck out like a snake, catching Cedar in the side of the head. As Cedar faltered to one side, Water whirled around to the other, and landed a second blow to his head. This time, however, he let the movement carry him until he had bowled the other trainee over. The two rolled in tandem, gripping each other's shoulders and trying to find purchase in the smooth ground. Water slammed Cedar into a rock jutting out of the moorland slopes and sprang away quickly, recovering.

"That's enough!" Fern raced over and stepped between them. "You fought dirtily, Water. We don't—"

"How can you expect our enemies to fight cleanly? Nicely, even? *Fairly?*" he defended himself hotly.

"He fought fine." Cedar came to stand at his side, staring at his instructor. "I'm not hurt, and I'd like to learn a few of his moves. They could be very useful in combat."

"What about when he slammed you onto that stone? That could have taken a turn for the worse if it had been your head instead of your back." Fern's face was creased with a mixture of worry and fear. "The last thing we need is a training accident."

"Look," Water began, "I know that that was wrong of me. I'll make sure to not go as hard."

"No, we want you to train your hardest and best, but it's your tactics that need to change. I've seen moves similar to those before, used by the exiles." As Water searched Fern's face, he was shocked to find a lingering distrust.

"Any exile in particular?" He glared at the older rabbit, but Fern was silent. "I *knew* it! I knew I'd never be able to be seen for who *I* am, and that when all of you look at me, you only see my father and my mother, and the crimes they have committed!"

"We don't see them," Root reasoned calmly, unbothered by the mounting chaos. "I'll tell you what I honestly see, if you want."

"Save it," Fern snapped. "A need for attention isn't hereditary, and *you've* proved that. If he wants to be his own rabbit, then he must earn the distinction.

But this session is over. Go show Water to his den and be quick about it."

Muttering crossly, Root fell into step behind Cedar and Boulder in the tunnel, while Water took up the rear. Once their instructors were far behind, Cedar dropped back to walk beside his littermate.

"What were you *thinking* back there? Another argument with Fern will land you in trouble again. What's it worth to anyone, anyway?"

She ignored his question. "It wasn't an argument, because he wouldn't let me get a word in at—"

"That's because he was telling you *off!* He's the instructor and you are the student, and so that's just how it works," Cedar spat.

"You're *just* like him, always interrupting me! Putting me off over and over again—I just won't have it! I want my say!"

"And you can have it without being rude!"

"I used to not be, you know? I used to keep my mouth shut and it made me unhappy. But I'm not doing that anymore, not if I respect myself at all, and *certainly* not if I respect the rest of you. It's hardly my fault if you and Fern shared the same faulty carrot and decide to snarl at me for it."

"Whatever, just stay out of trouble, you hear? It makes both of us look bad," Cedar said, barging ahead.

Root huffed, rolling her eyes. "What a lousy piece of work!"

"Don't you worry, I'll work on him a bit," Water joked. "Maybe if he hits that rock just right next time, it'll knock some sense into him."

"Not funny." Root shook her head.

"Then why are your whiskers twitching?" Water pointed out amiably.

"Because it shouldn't *be* funny."

He looked from side to side, then whispered, "But there's no one here to tell you to stop laughing, is there?"

"I don't suppose there is." She glanced back at him as they walked, eyes gleaming with amusement. "But Cedar's just jealous that I got Chill as my instructor and he didn't. I don't see why he should feel that way when Chill isn't even here to train me half the time. And he's not sick by the way, *or* staying in."

"Really? Where is he, then?" Water was puzzled.

"At the border, probably. He sulks around there all the time, like a big old stinking heap of misery. I found him there once and he looked like he was falling apart." She shrugged. "Or at least, he certainly isn't holding together."

"But why? Surely his time is more valuable than to waste just loitering about all day? He *is* Head Patroller," Water pointed out.

"I don't really know much about the matter, to be honest, but we could find out."

"*Spy on him?* How? We've got training every day. We couldn't spare the time."

"Well, we'd make something up, of course. I could tell Light that Chill wants to do a training bout with just the two of us, and we'd slip out. We would head directly for the border and search for him there. Then we could watch him."

"All right. Tomorrow, then?" Water checked.

"Tomorrow it is," Root agreed, excited by the prospect of danger and sneaking around. Water's stomach churned as his excitement shifted to uneasiness. *Is this a bad idea?*

CHAPTER FOUR

Wind hauled himself from his nest, over shredded bits of golden light on the floor of his den under the bramble thicket, telling him that the sun must already be well on its journey across the sky. He yawned, washed his pelt quickly, and pushed his way outside. He crossed the training clearing briskly and ducked under the ferns crowding the edges of the main camp. The whole space was alive with activity. Some rabbits groomed their fur or grazed quietly at the fringes of the camp, while others sparred to keep their skills sharp.

Two burly, male rivals tumbled past him in a blur of claws and fur. He continued on without a worry, making for the entrance.

"Wind! Where are you headed for?" Silver called to him, her white underbelly catching the sun as she lounged on her side against her den.

"Just out. I wanted to check for any colony rabbits who might have gotten lost or crossed our borders."

"Count me in." Silver climbed to her paws and stretched. "I'm just about itching for something to happen around here, and our campmates are being a little too good as of late."

"Hopefully because of my presence?"

She growled. "You couldn't startle a beetle. Let's get moving now."

He led the way, making a beeline for the border, which he knew was marked by the edge of the trees. He occasionally stopped briefly to scent the air, and Silver remained more patient than usual, lazily twitching her ears.

Suddenly her indifference evaporated at the snap of a twig from ahead, and she straightened her ears, eyes wide and alert. She motioned for him to follow as she crept along stealthily, carefully parting the bracken to reveal a little patch of barren ground where a single rabbit sat with his back to them and his head bowed over a mound of earth. He appeared to be grieving.

Wind's breath sped up with excitement, and as if sensing the subtle change in the air, the rabbit turned his head and peered into the bracken where they were hiding. Silver's breath caught in her throat, and she straightened up before strolling out and facing the stranger, a brown and white male.

"You are trespassing," she snarled.

"I am mourning," he replied. He took no defensive posture, but rather simply sat staring at them, as if stunned to see other rabbits. What was wrong with him? Was this what grief, or sentimentality, did to a rabbit? Broke them?

"There is a rule in place for both groups, and you have violated it."

"That was not my intent. I wish for peace, and that is all."

"Then don't bury your dead on our land, Chill!" she snapped.

He frowned. "I buried a rabbit I loved, so it does not matter where I go to grieve them. This place is peaceful, and she would've loved it here."

"I don't want to hear about your mate, Chill. I'm done caring about you or your life." Silver glared resentfully at him.

"She wasn't my mate." He stood up and shook out his fur, looking curiously at Silver. "I didn't give her that chance, to my everlasting regret." He stared down at the mound of earth that was encircled with stones. "I miss her terribly, but she is lost to me. I had many chances to speak up to her, but I never did. Now she's an exile, and I can't get her back. You both are lucky to have her in your group. I'll leave in a moment, if that's all right."

Silver shuddered. "Chill, look at me. Why are you acting like this?"

"Why do you keep speaking to me as if you know me?" Chill said in a flat voice, his brown gaze blank.

She stomped over and planted herself in front of the pile of dirt. "Because I *do* know you! Now what is this thing you've built?" She pawed at it.

"Be careful!" he warned. "It's a grave."

"For me? You buried me?" Her voice was sorrowful, and Wind reeled from the strangeness of hearing emotion from her.

"No." He looked confused. "For a rabbit named Silver. She died a while ago." He then grew frustrated. "Can you please leave me now? You are disrupting the peace. I have nothing to say to you. I don't know you."

"I *am* Silver, Chill," she fumed. "How can you not remember me? Your face is seared in my mind forever."

Recognition dawned on his face. "*Silver?* I did not know you for all of the scars you have. Even so, you are dead to me. I accepted that long ago."

"So I'm dead to you? That's just great, isn't it? Tell him how great that is, Wind!" She stalked off, anger tainting her scent trail.

Chill simply watched her leave. He turned his eyes on Wind. "You've grown so much."

"I had to. I'd be dead if I weren't big enough to fight, and strong enough to kill."

Chill pressed his eyes tightly shut. "How many have you killed?"

"Many. And I will add one more to that number right now if you don't get out of my territory and stay out of it."

"You would threaten me?"

"Is there a reason I shouldn't?"

"I'm your brother, from the same litter as Darkside. Did they not tell you about me, or the rest of us?"

"Both my parents were exiles. I had always assumed that was where I came from," Wind lied, hearing the taunts about being born into the colony ringing through his head. He shook himself to clear it before agitation welled up. "I have to go."

"All right." Chill turned back to the memorial. "There's no rush."

Without waiting around for anything else to happen, Wind darted away as if he was being chased. *If he's anything like Darkside, then I'm fortunate to not know him.*

* * *

Wind narrowed his eyes against the glare of the sun. He stepped back into the shade as Slicer and Dicer, the almost identical brown-and-white-patched littermates who had been exiled together for joint participation in serious crimes, each dipped their front paws in the cool water of the stream.

"Isn't it nice that we can just come here whenever we want? The tugging of the stream reminds me of the moorland breeze in my fur," Slicer said with a dreamy sigh. "What I wouldn't give to have that back!"

"I miss it, too," Dicer agreed. "How about a making a visit? Those lazy colony scum will never even know."

"I'd like that," Slicer said, her murky brown eyes glinting slyly. "Wind, will you be joining us?"

"I wouldn't miss it." He nodded.

"Lead the way?" Dicer stepped aside.

"Sure." He marched past them. They fell in behind him as he continued along the well-worn track.

"You know what? I know this really great spot. How about *I* lead the way so that I can show you both to it?" Slicer slipped ahead of Wind, but he only shrugged. She knew that he could stop her if he wanted to.

They successfully reached the border. He could hear the wind whipping and whistling against the barren landscape just ahead. His ears twitched toward it. He weaved past his fellow exiles and broke through the tree line. Wind snapped his eyes closed, and slowly reopened them to adjust to the sun-bleached world around him. He looked back, but Slicer and Dicer had vanished from view.

"Hey, you there! Stop!" an unfamiliar voice ordered.

CHAPTER FIVE

Water quietly followed Root from the tunnel, and they raced across the grass until they reached the shade of a boulder and rested briefly under it.

"So," he panted, "it's all set, then? Light thinks I'm out for a training session, right?"

"I think he savored the idea of having a day off," she sneered.

"Good. Now, where next?"

"It's this way." She motioned for him to follow, and together they bounded to the edge of the forest. "We'll cover more ground if we split up, all right? I say we go in opposite directions along the tree line and meet up here again at sunset. That's the entire day to search and collect information. But just be careful of the exiles," she said as she looked away.

"What?" he asked immediately. "I'll be fine."

"It's not that," she snapped. "You're not bothered by this at all? Being so close to your brother and mother?"

"Nettle is back in the tunnels, or training, and it's unlikely that I'll see Jo, and even more unlikely that she'd recognize me," he reasoned.

She sighed. "You were never meant to know this, but when I saw Chill sulking at the border the first time, he was talking out loud to himself. He said it was a mistake that 'those two kits were separated.' I confronted him about it later, and he finally told me that you have a brother named Wind who was sent away with Jo to the exiles."

"That's not true. You're making things up!"

Root cocked her head to one side and looked into his eyes.

"I'm sorry, Water. I know it must come as a shock, but it is true."

"But why would they do that to us? How could they lie to me like that? I have to find him and tell him!"

"Water, you can't." Root blocked his path. "He is an *exile*. That means that he was raised to kill and lie and fight. He's dangerous. It won't be the big reunion that you're imagining. Just don't get yourself mixed up in that, okay? I'll see you at sunset." She gazed grimly at him before turning and hopping away.

My brother, Wind. Taken. Made an exile.

Water felt the emptiness inside of him grow, as if it's hunger for satisfaction had intensified.

Water shook his head angrily before trudging the other way. He picked his way through the debris by the forest when a figure melted out of the shadows and stalked into the open, where it stood, legs splayed arrogantly, head high, and broad shoulders set firmly.

His anger mounted. Whoever the stranger was, he had picked the wrong day to cross the border and to cross Water's path. Water charged at the exile trespasser, yelling for him to halt for a confrontation.

The sturdy, light gray male jerked his head around to take him in, blue eyes widened with surprise.

"You thought you could get away with trespassing, you disgusting, traitorous outcast!" Water bellowed. He leapt at the exile and they rolled together, equals in size and strength. They grappled, clawing at one another, but Water felt uneasy.

He had never seen an exile before, but now he knew why all of his friends feared them. Were all exiles this huge? Just a group of massive, savage brutes who liked to kill?

He was kicked away, and both stood facing each other, breathing heavily and with fur scuffed up from the fight, their shoulders hunched and chests heaving. Water was beginning to regret his hotheadedness. Why had he decided to try and pick a fight with this killer, who must have much more experience and sneaky tricks?

"Get off my land," he panted.

"*Make* me."

"Listen here, you poor excuse for a creature—"

"That's an *awfully* long name. Colony rabbits sure are strange." The gray rabbit sat down complacently and stared at him. "How about you tell your pathetic friends back in their pampered nests that they can call me Wind."

"Wind? Not the… not son of Billy and Jo?" Water murmured aloud, dazed.

"Oh? You've heard of me, then?" The exile seemed satisfied. "Great, then forget about telling all of your friends, as I'm sure you've already gotten out all of your scary stories of me."

"The only thing that would scare them is how ugly you are. You look like a slug in a drought."

"Hey! Who do you think you are, talking to me like that? I'll show you how fast this slug moves, and once I've pinned you down, you'll *have* to tell me who you are so I can brag about chasing you off!"

"You'll have to catch me first!" Water dived to the side and sprinted away, Wind on his heels. He rounded a boulder and ended up chasing his former pursuer. Wind slammed to a stop and they collided under the shade of an overhanging rock, legs tangled.

"You should've seen your face when I got behind you! No kit in the entire colony would ever fall for that trick!" he crowed, laughing.

Wind pounced on him and held him down, but Water was reassured to see that Wind had no intention of hurting him, exhilarated from the short sprint. "I win! Now, tell me who you are."

"My name is Water."

Wind looked at him blankly. "Is that supposed to mean something to me? I've never heard of you."

"We're littermates. We were separated at birth."

Wind laughed.

"I have no littermates! No brothers! I am an exile. You can drop the sad separated-at-birth story too, because I've had sentimentality trained out of me!" Wind puffed out his chest, letting him get up.

"Then enlighten me: you seemed to have been having fun in that game of chase, and you just set a rival free. Why?" Water asked.

"I was trying to get information, not play, and I let you go because I *felt* like it."

"But isn't that sentimentality? You wouldn't have let any other enemy go. What makes me so special to you?"

"You were honest with me, and I could tell that you didn't want to injure me," Wind confessed. "I've never seen a rabbit be completely honest if it wasn't for their own gain, and even then, what they said or did was never completely true. I respect that."

"Of course. Meet me here tomorrow night so can we discuss this more, all right?"

"Why should I?"

"You know why. Meet me *right here,*" Water asked without thinking.

"Okay, fine. I'll be waiting for you," Wind promised. "Will you be able to get here?"

"It might take a few lies here and there, but nothing is without risk." He shrugged. "And it's not like we're doing any rabbit any harm, right?"

"Yeah, well, if what you say is true, then they *owe* this to you, for lying about us being separated. It'll be easy for me to get away, since none of the other exiles dares to face me," Wind pronounced smugly. "Hey, how'd you find out about it, anyways?"

A call sounded from across the moorland. "Water? Where are you? It's getting dark!" It was Root, eyes sweeping the land for him. Her dark ginger-and-white pelt stuck out like the wings of a monarch butterfly against the grass.

"I have to go, but I'll explain to you tomorrow about that," Water promised.

"I look forward to it." Wind scampered off, disappearing into the dark forest. By the time Root had spotted and reached Water, his brother's scent had been abraded by the harsh, cold winds.

CHAPTER SIX

The following night, Wind crept from his den, scanning the darkness for any other rabbits who might try to hold him back. He finally bounded quickly across the training clearing and set paw in the ferns, ducking low.

"Hello, Wind." He jumped at Silver's voice from the entrance to her den, where she sat as unmoving as a stone. They hadn't spoken since she had stormed away from Chill, from her grave site.

"Silver. I was just going out to the stream for a drink, and I also wanted to explore the territory on my own to see what it looks like at night. I might not be back until morning."

"Then do yourself a favor: don't sneak out or around. You are the second-in-command here, so you've no reason to creep past those weaklings."

"I didn't mean for it to appear that way," he told her rapidly.

“You need to know something, Wind.” Silver froze him with a glare. “I do not, and will *not* tolerate a rabbit holding a secret over me. I have entrusted you with your rank, and as the higher power in this camp, I order you to forget what you witnessed two days ago in that clearing by the border. It is a part of your oath to be loyal to me, so you will never speak of that, do you hear?”

“Yes. I would never tell any rabbit that, and never will,” he swore. “I’ll be on my way now, if you don’t mind.”

“In a hurry?”

“Uh—no. I just want plenty of time to look around.”

“Enjoy the stream. But be careful, it’s easy to slip in when it’s so dark.” She narrowed her eyes meaningfully and vanished into her den.

Releasing the breath he had been holding, Wind hurried out of camp. He skimmed through the shadows and his ears swiveled around at every slight noise. Even the toughest and strongest exiles were wary of venturing out into the forest at night, unwilling to pay the risk of being outnumbered by their own campmates and killed in silence. They would never return to camp, and that was fine, so long as no rabbit asked or told. There was at least some decency inside the protective walls of the camp.

His breathing quickened as he neared the invisible border line, where the trees cut off to the moorland, where the envious exiles, lurking in the condemned shadows, watched the colony rabbits who had tossed them aside running freely and joyously with the wind in their ears. He felt a growl rumble in his throat, but silenced it quickly. He was here on friendly terms. He had been invited by his brother, Water.

Wind looked about him in wonder at the moonlit sweep of hills as he approached the meeting place, transfixed by its gleaming silver grass and how the boulders seemed to sparkle under the dim light. He could see his own paws for once, as they were not covered by leaves or twigs as they were in the forest.

That was when he looked up, and gasped. The sky, which he rarely saw, as it was always blocked out by tree branches and leaves, was a vast expanse of stars that crowded one another for room. It looked like the moonlight had exploded into countless embers.

Tearing his eyes away and fixing them on the path at his paws, he hurried toward the rocky overhang, where Water peeled away from the shadows and came to greet him.

His brother stopped just a few strides away from the shelter and looked around. "I saw how you looked at the moorland just now. I could tell you were fascinated by it. I now realize just how much I've taken this territory for granted."

"Hopefully we can realize more of these things together," he urged.

"I'd like that," Water murmured. "I feel dreadful that you had to be sent away to live with those criminals while I got to stay here, to stay safe. The wind doesn't deserve to be trapped among the trees. You should be out here with me. You *could* be out here with me, if you wanted to," he added hopefully.

"It's not that simple." Wind looked away with a sigh. "Nothing has ever been simple."

He let Water lead him across to the rocky overhang, where they sat down together and gazed out over the landscape.

"Maybe there was a point in time where I could've returned, and would have been welcomed, but that time did not last. You have to understand that I am not innocent anymore, Water. I'm the second-in-command of the exiles. Rank does not come without action."

"So?" Water stared at him. "You don't owe them anything! You can come home, where you *belong*."

"Look," Wind began, an edge to his words, "I had to *kill* other rabbits to achieve my position. I might as well stay there, since I have done these things."

"You killed other *exiles*." Water tipped his head to one side. "Most of them have done worse."

"No, I killed another kit who was just trying to survive like me. He had never done anything wrong, but that's not even the worst part." Water was silent, allowing Wind to gather himself back up before continuing.

"I'm being trained to kill, Water. Silver, my leader, wants me to practice this not only on my campmates, but also on colony rabbits who stray past the border or who are alone." Wind shuddered. "I don't want to talk about this anymore. Tell me about your training."

"It's all right. I'm a Patroller, and my instructor is named Light."

"And what do you think of him?"

Water snorted. "He's too controlling over every other rabbit, even though he's always so jumpy. I get the idea that he has no clue how to train me. I just wish that I had gotten an instructor with a little more experience, you know?"

"Why were you given an inexperienced instructor? Is someone trying to hold you back?"

"I don't know, but I feel like Deerface lets the other three leaders make all of the decisions, even though their minds are addled by age. He's too afraid to contradict them, even on what they eat, I'd bet!" Water huffed.

"What would *you* do differently?"

"Me? Well, I wouldn't be afraid to be different from my peers or equals. I would face any problems head-on, instead of just dancing around them."

"It sounds like you'd make a great leader someday. Have you ever thought about it?"

"Not *really*. I mean, I think I could do more good. I've been too busy to actually consider it," Water confessed as he frowned in thought.

"Then you should do everything you can to become leader. Deerface is obviously a coward," Wind stated smartly.

Water threw him a sidelong glance. "Deerface is our brother, but he and his mate, Blizzard, raised me."

"That's perfect! Since you are so close to Deerface and Blizzard, you should be able to get them to notice you. Try to put the idea of promoting you into

Blizzard's head, and she'll mention it to Deerface if she agrees with you."

Water was nodding. "That could work. I'll try it sometime. Hey, thanks."

"No problem. I should go soon, but I've enjoyed our talk. When can we meet again?"

"You'd want to?" Water gazed at him with relief in his eyes.

"Of course. I've never had another rabbit that I could be so open with, and I honestly don't think that I ever will," Wind said warmly as he nudged his littermate.

"You'll always have me. Nothing will ever come between us, between this, I promise. Let's meet in three days, at midnight. I don't want my denmates to get suspicious, and I have to keep up with my sleep," Water explained. "See you then?"

"I'll be here," Wind agreed happily.

CHAPTER SEVEN

Water reached the tunnel back at the warren and ducked into it, feeling light with joy after his third secret meeting with Wind. Their meetings were becoming increasingly frequent. He turned his paws toward his den.

"Water? What are you doing up so late?" Bramble faced him reproachfully.

He looked up. "I-I haven't been. I just woke up and went for a drink at the stream."

"By the border?" Bramble's eyes narrowed with suspicion. "You should be more careful. The exiles would tear you to shreds so much as look at you, or just for fun."

A knot of frustration flared up in Water's chest at this common bias, and his claws sunk into the ground to suppress it. "But is that true for *all* exiles? Surely some of them are different?"

Bramble narrowed his eyes. "Why do you think they were exiled in the first place?"

"I'm just saying that maybe not all of them are guilty. Kits are born within that camp, the generations are replenished over time, and maybe some of them were even wrongfully convicted. Why should *they* receive such scorn, as well, when they are not at fault?"

"Because they are just like their parents! Worse, even. Every one of *our* generations evolves, gets better. Theirs does the opposite. They become more evil. It's just in their blood," Bramble snarled.

"So you think it's in my blood, as well? The desire to kill?" Water silently dared him to agree.

"I'll tell you what I think: you don't belong here, and why the leaders decided to keep you here is beyond me. I know that others feel the same." Bramble raised his chin haughtily.

Water felt his heart shrink. Was this really true? Did *everyone* hate him?

Suddenly, a shadow tackled Bramble and pinned him to the ground, leaning in close with a snarl. "How dare you concoct such lies about my student!"

"Light! Get off of me!"

Light shoved him away with another snarl of warning. "Keep your mouth shut, Bramble. Unless you think that all of Billy's kits don't belong here?"

"This doesn't concern Deerface *or* Chill," Bramble snarled.

"It will if you keep this up," Light threatened. "I know about what you were saying the other day to the other Patrollers."

"I have no idea what you're talking about! I say tons of things to the other Patrollers, since we all *work* together!"

"Don't play dumb. I've been investigating you for long enough to know that you're trying to get Billy's kits kicked across the border, starting with Water and Nettle."

"Nettle?" Water took a step toward them. "What does Nettle have to do with anything? Don't you *dare* involve him in this!"

Bramble looked back at him and sneered, "What do you care? He's not the brother that matters to you anyway."

"Enough!" Light stepped off Bramble, who righted himself and shook out his fur. He stood glowering for a few seconds more.

"Do yourself a favor and stay out of this, Light. This goes much deeper than just a few conversations. Eventually, everything leads back to Billy." Bramble turned away abruptly and stalked off down the tunnel.

Light was silent for a few moments, but then he fixed his pale, grayish-green gaze on Water. "There are things we need to discuss, and it might take an entire day to get through them. Come with me."

He headed back outside, and they went to sit on the crest of a hill, facing the rising sun. "I've been investigating Bramble for as long as I can remember, ever since I had found out that he had a secret and personal connection to Billy. After Billy's death, I thought that he had cut ties with the exiles."

"He was working for my father?" Water gasped.

"At one point in time, yes. I had requested to train you so that I could get closer to him to figure out what he had done for Billy, and also because I had suspected he would come after you."

"I would have just fought him off. I'm bigger and stronger than he is." Water sat up taller and raised his chin defiantly.

Light shook his head. "I don't think he's alone. Anyway, I put a few things together, and I paid a visit to Billy's grave. I caught many scents there, his mingled with exile scents. I believe he used to meet Billy in that spot, and now he's meeting with the other exiles there. I think he wants to get all of Billy's kin exiled so that they can all fight for their father's group and carry out his plans. He wants Billy's *family* there, because they are more likely to stick together than a bunch of criminals."

"He can't!" Water jumped to his paws. "How do we stop him? Can't we talk to Deerface about this?"

"Not until we know more. This is a sensitive subject for Deerface, one would think. Tell me, what did Bramble mean when he said those things about Nettle?"

Water felt a hard knot grow in his stomach. "I have no idea! It was probably just a lie to throw you off. If I knew what he had meant by it, you'd be the first to know."

Light's eyes were sharp with intelligence as he studied Water. "I hope that's true, because this is bigger than just us. I want to know what those mangy exiles are planning. The borders have been very quiet recently, which has me worried. It isn't in their nature to be quiet."

"Maybe they're just nervous after the battle where Billy was killed."

"Or maybe it's a new leadership. Could the problem be coming from there? Maybe we need to convince our leaders to take out theirs."

"That's way too risky," he said rapidly, steering the focus away from Wind and the prospect of harming him, though Wind was capable of protecting himself. "Let's just wait for them to make the next move. Who knows, this new leadership could be making the exiles less interested in picking fights." He felt a growing sense of urgency, partly relieved to know that he would see Wind again that night.

"Fine, but that just leaves me with more questions. Take the day off today, all right? But remember to be vigilant. I'll see you tomorrow." Light frowned distractedly before heading back across the moorland in search of a quiet place to think.

Water released a huge breath, relieved but nervous that Light was investigating. A rabbit as intelligent as he was sure to get to the bottom of everything quickly. Maybe Light had put up a front with him at first, but now Water had a completely altered perspective of his instructor. He respected Light for wanting to solve these problems, but he couldn't agree that he should suggest attacking his brother. *But he doesn't know about Wind.*

Water wandered over to a boulder and tilted his head back, but could not see the top clearly. He put his paws against the side and hauled himself up, paw by paw. He grunted with the effort, until he had scrambled to the smooth top. He could see a lot more from this vantage point, including his meeting place with Wind.

"Hey there, Water. What brings you here?" He recognized Root's voice before he even turned around to see his ginger-and-white denmate. Taken by surprise, he lost his balance and his paws skidded out from under him. He slithered toward the edge, clawing frantically for a grip.

Teeth connected in his scruff and pulled him back toward the center of the massive rock.

"Thanks," he mumbled to Root.

She shrugged. "What brings you here?"

"Er… Light gave me the day off, so I just wanted to clear my head."

"You can't really do that if it's splattered all over the grass. You should be more careful," she told him, eyes gleaming with amusement.

He ducked his head in embarrassment, then changed the subject by asking, "Why are *you* here?"

"It's kind of my place. I like the view, and I can also spy on Chill from here."

"Really?" He looked down toward the tree line.

"Yeah. He does all *sorts* of interesting things." She settled down and let her front paws dangle over the edge distractedly.

"Like what?" he asked curiously.

"Oh, sometimes he climbs the trees and swings from branch to branch, and other times he grows wings and flies up to eat the clouds." She rolled her eyes and nudged him. "Haven't I already told you that he just sits there and mopes all day long? You moron."

"Hey, you're the one who decided to spy on him, so you can't expect him to do tricks to entertain you all the while." He nudged her back. "Mind if I sit?"

"Why not? But be careful, because I once knew this rabbit named Water who almost fell off a boulder and died. Luckily for him, I was there."

"Very funny." He lay down and looked out over the treetops. The sun-warmed rock felt wonderful, and he relaxed his entire body into it. He was just starting to doze off when Root prodded him hard in the shoulder.

"Look!" He followed her gaze to where Deerface was padding along the border quietly, listening to Stewie ramble on about random subjects. "He must be taking her out to get some fresh air. I heard she was very frail these days, but I found that hard to imagine, until now!"

"Poor Stewie. She mustn't get out much these days. She's a very loyal and trustworthy rabbit, once you get around her quick temper," he murmured.

"Yeah, I like that about her. You can always trust her to tell you how she really feels, no matter if that's what you'd like to hear or not!" Root laughed.

"A lot like you." Water glanced sideways at her.

"You little weasel! If death wasn't just a misstep away, I'd pop you one for that," she huffed.

Water snorted, secretly admiring her boldness. Root was not easily intimidated and had a lot of spirit.

Together they watched as Deerface and Stewie walked past, almost close enough to brush against the rock that they were lounging on top of. Their voices drifted up to them as both leaders stopped to take a brief rest.

"I'm not *saying* that, Stewie. I'm just suggesting that you retire. Continuing your duties can't be good for you. Please, let us take care of you," Deerface implored.

"My only retirement is death, kit."

"Don't say that!" Deerface recoiled at her bluntness.

"Too late. Let's get back so that I can sleep. All of this arguing is making my head spin." Stewie rose shakily to her paws, and Deerface escorted her away.

"Did you hear that?" Water asked.

"I sure did. Do you know what this means?" Root turned to him urgently. "If Stewie agrees to retire, then a spot as one of the leaders is open, and every rabbit is looking at you, Water."

"I don't want Stewie to die," he protested.

"I know, but you don't have to. She'll eventually have to retire. By the time she does, you'll be done training. Deerface would be insane to not promote you."

"It's not just Deerface's decision. Spatula and Runt have a say in it, too," he insisted.

"Spatula and Stewie are the same age, and Runt isn't too far behind. They'll retire together, and Deerface will need to fill in their places quickly. You should go talk to him, ease him into the idea. I'll come, if you want."

"All right, but only because I want to check in on Runt and Spatula, as well. Do *not* mention promotions, clear?" He gazed at her seriously.

"Very," she agreed quickly, springing to her paws.

"Then let's hurry up," he sighed, and together they made their way down the boulder and started for the tunnels.

CHAPTER EIGHT

Wind glanced up. The moon was directly overhead. Where was Water? He started to pace back and forth in front of the boulder that marked their usual meeting place, until heavy breathing and the pounding of paws over grass announced his littermate's arrival.

"Sorry," Water panted, the moonlight glancing softly off of his heaving, silvery-blue shoulders. "I lost track of time, but I have good news."

Wind pricked up his ears. "What is it?"

"Root helped me to put the idea of promoting me into Deerface's head. She was great, very persuasive. I think he's actually considering it, thanks to her."

"Oh, that's great." He frowned. "But who's Root?"

Water traced a paw through the dirt, making a circle. "Just another Patroller that I sometimes train with. She's helping me investigate her instructor, Chill, and what he's been doing at the border."

"Chill? He's grieving, or so he says. He made a grave site for my leader, Silver, because he told her that she was dead to him for becoming an exile. He was friendly to me, though."

"When did the two of you speak?" Water leaned forward with interest.

Wind shifted his paws. "Not too long ago. Just before you and I met."

"Why didn't you tell me this earlier? We met over four weeks ago."

"It never crossed my mind. I had no reason to think it was important."

Water looked thoughtful. "If Root and I could help Chill to recover from this somehow, then it would look good in the sight of my leaders. Will you help me?"

"Of course," Wind agreed immediately.

"Thanks. So, what do you suggest we do?"

"Hmm..." Wind was silent as he contemplated it. "Darkside once told me that the only two things keeping a rabbit going are fear and fighting. What if I pretended to attack you and Root at the border, close by where Chill usually sits? He'll be sure to hear the commotion and will run to protect you two. I'll retreat, and maybe the scuffle will snap him out of it."

"That's brilliant, Wind!" Water congratulated him. "The end of my training is near, so I really need to do something to stand out. Can we do this tomorrow afternoon?"

"Sure. But what about your instructor?"

"We have an understanding on a few things. I'll tell him that I was following a lead."

"Good. I'll wait close by, and you two start heading toward Chill. But Root can't know, all right? I don't trust her, even if you do. Plus, she'll think you saved her."

"No way. I'm sorry, Wind, but I just can't lie to her. She needs to know."

"Fine," Wind snapped, turning away frostily. "But just remember who you're doing this for."

Water ducked his head. "I'm sorry, Wind. Root means a lot to me."

"Apparently *more* to you than I do."

"The relationships are incomparable," Water explained firmly, sounding slightly irritated.

"Whatever. I'm only saying that no matter what either of us means to you, you only have a certain amount of time each day, which can't be evenly divided between both of us, as well as your duties. I'll see you tomorrow." Before his brother could reply, Wind whirled around angrily and stalked off into the woods of the exile land, *his* land.

He marched right through cobwebs and bushes, unbothered as thorns dragged against his fur, scraping his skin. When he was nearing the camp, he slowed to a stop and caught his breath. His scratches from blundering through the forest started to sting dimly. He felt guilty for trying to make his brother give up another completely different relationship for theirs, but he put on an emotionless mask as he strutted into the camp.

"Where have you been?" Viper, ears low and eyes wide with anxiety, questioned him. Oddly, no rabbits were fighting, which was most unusual. All were quietly talking in small groups with heads close, casting tense glances at the rock that was Silver's den. "Silver has been looking everywhere for you. I think she got word from our allies in the colony, and it means trouble."

CHAPTER NINE

Water stuck his head around the corner, then beckoned to Root. "Come on! It's this way." He waited for her to catch up so that they could walk side by side down into the tunnel.

"Are you sure about this, Water? What if Wind doesn't keep his promise? He could really hurt us."

"He won't hurt us. I trust him. Besides," he added, "this could be the only way to help Chill. And to my understanding, you've never minded taking risks or sneaking around."

"I hope that you're right about Wind. And I only like the thrill of sneaking around if I don't have the possibility of getting killed, or of *you* getting killed. I can bear having to clean out the dens or having to eat last," she said, averting her eyes from his.

They exited the tunnels. "Light will think that I've either gotten confused and gone somewhere else, or that I'm just out for a break," Water said, reassuring her.

"What if more exiles follow Wind?" she asked him worriedly.

"They won't. Wind doesn't really have any buddies among the exiles that he hangs out with or trusts. He's all alone there."

"I suppose you're right. So when he jumps out at us, and after Chill comes, I say that you saw him about to attack me at the border, and that you were trying to fight him off?"

"Yes, that's perfect."

They walked a while until they eventually reached the shady tree line and quickly followed it until they were close enough to Chill's usual grieving place to see glimpses of his brown-and-white pelt through the trees. Water looked about until he was staring into two piercing, familiar blue eyes.

Wind exploded from the woods with a fearsome snarl, lips peeled back and claws at the ready. For a fleeting moment, Water understood Root's fear of his brother.

Water caught his brother softly and they rolled, faking swipes and their teeth snapping close enough to one another that any observer would think it was real.

Root added to the effect of the ploy by emitting a shocked screech.

It wasn't long before Chill skidded around the bend and froze with horror. He then tried to force himself between them, and Water let himself be knocked roughly away. Wind tumbled to a stop nearby and growled menacingly at them, eyes darting triumphant glances at Water, who nodded in return.

"What's going on here?" Chill glared at Wind.

"That exile ambushed Root when she was checking the borders, and I rushed over to try and drive him off. If you hadn't come when you did, this could've ended very badly." Water curled his lip pointedly.

"He saved me from being ripped to shreds by that savage," Root added, eyes wide.

"Really?" Chill tipped his head at Water. He shook out his fur, then puffed out his chest like a student who had just received a compliment from his instructor, before stating, "Well, it's my duty to protect my colony mates, and I'm sure that Wind can find his way back to his own territory. By which I mean right *now.*"

Wind lowered his head, eyes vicious as he growled, "This isn't over, you colony *filth*! Keep looking over your shoulders, because when you don't, I'll be there, and *you'll* be dead!" Without another word, he then turned on his paws and raced for the trees.

"Thank you again, Chill. I don't know what we'd have done if you hadn't been nearby. We should go report this to Deerface. Will you lead?"

With a purposeful nod, Chill marched across the hills on the path to the burrows, with Water and Root in tow. He talked as they went.

"I haven't seen an exile attack so pointed and vicious since the Great Ambush, but that seems like it was ages ago." A haunted look crept into Chill's eyes.

"I remember. It was right after I received my blessing," Root murmured with a shiver.

"I've only ever heard little bits and pieces about it, not ever really enough to put it all together." Water tipped his head to one side as he gazed at Chill. "What happened, exactly? Every rabbit is too afraid to talk about it."

"Well," Chill hesitated, "I remember that Darkside appeared at the border to surrender to Deerface, but when Darkside tackled Deerface, Billy's armies ambushed the rest of us. It was a very bloody battle, since the exiles were fighting to kill. Many died from both sides, but it was Billy's death that finally caused the exiles to retreat. Deerface did what he had to do, killing Billy."

"I've never understood that part. He was our father. How could Deerface *do* that? I heard that Billy just wanted all of his family together."

"You never met Billy." Chill gazed steadily at him. "He was *ruthless*. All he wanted was an excuse to kill, and that was what we became to him."

"I wish I could've met him. Maybe I could have made him see sense," Water murmured wistfully.

Chill shook his head sadly. “No rabbit could have done that, Water. Billy was just… evil. But I’ve learned that we don’t have to be like our father. We have a chance to do what he could never do: be happy without using cruelty, as well as with where we stand, as long as we are helping our colony, that is.”

“But I have ambitions as well,” Water confessed. “Billy was the same. Doesn’t that mean—”

“Just drop it, Water. Bringing up Billy’s past won’t solve any of our problems.” Chill sighed wearily, an edge of warning bleeding into his tone.

“Even when all of our problems lead back to him?” Water muttered almost inaudibly.

“What is *that* supposed to mean?” Chill turned on him, a deeply disturbed frown creasing his face.

“Nothing. I was just thinking out loud. Forget I said anything.” Water shifted uncomfortably as Chill stared at him, but refused to break his gaze. The Head Patroller snorted, shook his head, and ducked into the tunnel that led to the Ceremonial Cavern.

Inside, Deerface and Spatula were coaxing Stewie to eat a small pile of grass, but she was proving to be stubborn. Runt paced off to one side, radiating irritation from his sharp gaze and stocky movements.

Chill cleared his throat, and four surprised gazes snapped toward him.

"Chill!" Deerface trotted over and touched his nose to Chill's shoulder briefly before looking him in the eyes. "I'm happy to see you again. No rabbit ever sees you anymore."

"I needed a little time to myself." Chill looked uncomfortable. "I just happened to hear these two being attacked at the border by an exile, and you'll never guess who." Chill's eyes glinted.

"I might have a few names in mind." Deerface flitted a worried glance at Water. "Was it Darkside?"

"No. It was Wind." Chill's expression was insistent as he watched Deerface, who quickly frowned, troubled.

"You're sure it was him?" Spatula asked, as if filled with dread.

"Yes. Now, I'd like to speak to the three of you in private, please." Chill glanced pointedly at Root and Water.

"Leave us." Deerface appeared to be deep in thought.

Water guided Root to a veering side passage and stopped.

"C'mon, let's go," Root huffed.

"No, I want to hear what Chill thinks is so private," Water whispered. He angled his ears to where Chill's insistent voice carried to them and crept forward to peek around the corner.

"Deerface, there is something that worries me beyond the exile attack from Wind."

Runt groaned, "Just when I thought we had had enough problems to deal with!"

"On the way here from the border, Water randomly started asking me the most bizarre questions about Billy and about the exiles. He started comparing himself to Billy in ways that I found worrisome. Then, when I told him to leave it alone, he said something under his breath, and I honestly don't think I was meant to hear it. He said that 'all things lead back to Billy,' and when I *confronted* him about it, he stayed silent. The way he looked at me after that, all furious and defiant, it kind of scared me."

Deerface stared hard at his littermate for a few long seconds, eyes slightly narrowed. "What are you implying, Chill?"

"I'm not *implying* anything, I'm reporting." Chill gazed evenly at Deerface. "That's the job of the Head Patroller, or am I wrong?"

"You've been gone so much, you could have forgotten. Tell me, what exactly have you been doing all this time?"

Chill looked shocked and furious. "What are *you* implying? How could you question me? I'm your brother!"

"As is Water," Deerface countered, watching Chill cautiously.

"That's not my point! I've have been trying to figure out what's up and what's down, and suddenly *I'm* a traitor?"

"You don't think that students like Water aren't trying to figure things out the same as you? And you *have* betrayed your colony, by neglecting your duties to it for your own self-conflicts. Which, luckily for you, in not a crime punishable by exile."

"Well, maybe we shouldn't let corrupt rabbits have high positions." Chill let his gaze sweep around the room. "So, how will you punish me for the *neglect of my duties?*"

Deerface turned away. "Like you said, we are brothers. Carry on with your work and this can rest."

"I accept that, but there is also something, a precaution, I think we should take. Water—"

"Just leave that kit alone, Chill!" Deerface snarled.

Chill spoke more quietly. "If Water is as good as you say, then we cannot spoil that. I believe that his instructor is corrupting him. Light is a young, easily manipulated rabbit who could have been swayed by Billy's followers. It would be easy for him to trick Water."

Once more, Deerface was frowning in thought. "Light isn't stupid."

Chill stepped urgently toward Deerface. "That's why he would be able to blend in with us! Don't you see? We cannot take the risk of giving him the chance to turn Water against us. Assign Water a different instructor."

"I can't fully take into consideration what you are proposing when your previous accusation is still so fresh in my mind. We will think carefully about this, then make the final decision. Leave us."

Looking hesitant with inner conflict, as if he thought he could say more to persuade Deerface, Chill finally turned away abruptly and marched off.

Deerface sighed. "I don't know how to deal with him. If I help him, he says I'm giving him special treatment. If I don't help him, he says I'm ignoring our kinship. But where in him did the urge to accuse Water of being a traitor *come* from?"

"I don't know where or what comes from any of you kits anymore," Stewie grumbled. "One of the reasons I'm glad I'm going deaf in my old age!"

"One of?" Deerface switched from distraught to amused. "How many reasons do you have, exactly?"

"Say it again?" Stewie tipped her head toward him.

Deerface chuffed. "Never mind."

Stewie sat back in satisfaction. "Good."

"Your ear fur is all matted again." Spatula was sniffing at Stewie's ears. "If we clean it up, you would be able to hear just fine."

"Oh, no, that's fine. I like it like this." Stewie wandered away.

"Okay, let's go before Stewie has the miracle of hearing us!" Water motioned for Root to follow as he broke into a run down the passage.

CHAPTER TEN

Wind headed through the trees to the border, hardly knowing what to expect from Water's plan. He couldn't help but recall his littermate's biting words: *I'm sorry, Wind. Root means a lot to me.*

He felt disturbed as he crouched in the undergrowth to wait, watching silently, although his mind was racing.

Am I losing him? He refused to do something for me because of her. He growled softly to himself. *She will not come between us. We promised each other that nothing ever will. After all, I am leaving this awful impression with the colony rabbits just to make him look good. This had better work.*

Then he spotted them: Two silhouettes descending from the crest of the hill. He recognized Water immediately, but he was left to assume that the second rabbit, a dark ginger female with brown eyes, was Root. She gazed about warily, occasionally looking to Water, who gave reassurance in the tiniest of nods and glances. Wind felt a sickening pang of jealousy of their obvious connection.

Suddenly his eyes locked with Water's—blue meeting amber, both intense with recognition and an understanding like no other. *How could I ever doubt him? No mere rabbit could ever separate this.*

Without any further hesitation, Wind burst his cover and tackled Water to the ground. They sparred like two kits would in the den, with nothing but an immense desire to prove themselves, even if the simple play seemed vicious.

As they tumbled about, Wind felt something in the pit of his stomach flare up. His chest tightened in response, pushing back, trying to quench what had become a desire to kill. His mind was frantic, his instincts screaming at him to draw blood, if only to see if this rabbit's was similar to his own. His eyes bored into Water's, but before his brother noticed the change in his demeanor, he was abruptly knocked away. Relief flooded Wind. Water could never know that Wind had wanted to kill him, if only in the heat of the moment, the thick of the fight. It had felt so real.

Wind rolled away in an advanced battle maneuver and ended neatly on his paws, bearing his head low with a fake snarl. He felt lighter to see pride and gratitude in Water's face.

"What's going on here?" Chill stared at Wind, as if shocked and wounded to find them like this. He had believed in Wind, but Wind had obliterated that for the chance of pleasing his more immediate brother. He suddenly felt weary, despondent as Water and Root balanced accusations on his hunched, tired shoulders.

Wind shook himself, remaining on guard as his narrowed eyes flickered from one colony rabbit to the next. He remembered what his campmates would always snarl when they boasted stories of chasing off colony rabbits, and repeated their words, "This isn't over, you colony *filth*! Keep looking over your shoulders, because when you don't, I'll be there, and *you'll* be dead!"

Wind turned tail and fled, thundering into the woods. He felt empty once more, but right now his brother would never find the time to schedule a meeting to talk. *I'd do anything for him, so why does this feel like he's only willing to do whatever is safest for him and Root?* Then he realized. *It's because I'm an exile. I can take those risks because I don't have to answer to anybody, except for Silver. Every one of his actions is monitored and picked apart by dozens of rabbits, most of which he doesn't even know at all.*

"I watched you fighting those mangy colony weasels, Wind. Most impressive." A huge, white male rabbit gave a grudging nod of admiration as he approached him head-on, unintimidated. "I'm Hemlock. I wanted to introduce you to a few of my friends, as it appears you don't have very many allies here."

Wind snorted. "And what is your gain from that, exactly?"

Hemlock's eyes glinted dangerously. "Another *friend.* I know who you are, or more importantly, I knew who you are related to. Billy and I consulted a lot, as I was in his inner circle. But the other members are dead. Crash, Adder, and Bark were killed in the same battle as Billy. Timber and I are still alive, while Stride and Buzzard have sworn allegiance to this group. Perhaps you'd like to attend one of our meetings, to see if joining us is in your future?"

"Meetings are for colony rabbits." Wind stalled, part of him hoping that Hemlock would insist and persuade him otherwise.

"No, meetings are for assurance of loyalty. We fight for each other, and that is our advantage over the other exiles, that is our key to survival. Billy originally formed this group in hopes that this strong, center alliance would rule supreme and force others to follow."

"Where is this meeting?" Wind asked, letting Hemlock claim what had already been won: his interest.

Hemlock looked pleased. "Follow me."

He set off at an unbothered pace, veering off the path to the camp, deeper into the woods. Hemlock seemed perfectly comfortable and confident off the trail, and sped forward to a small grove with looming oak trees on all sides. Sounds would not carry easily past the closely crowding trunks and the thick wall of ferns and weeds. Branches crisscrossed far above, so only small beams of light leaked through to the mostly barren forest floor.

"Hemlock! Where'd you go?" A black-furred male rabbit peeled away from the shadows and approached them. He looked Wind up and down, expressionless, as if waiting for an introduction.

"Buzzard, go fetch Timber and Stride. It's time to begin the meeting," Hemlock ordered instead of answering.

"I'm already here," growled a stocky, dark brown rabbit with a scratched-up muzzle and one cloudy white eye, following Buzzard over to them. His one good eye was a sharp, imposing green. "And I have Stride keeping watch close by, but he should still be able to hear us well enough. Is this him?" He narrowed his eyes at Wind.

"Yes," Hemlock said with triumph.

"Good. Billy always wanted for you to be one of us, but he expected to be here for that day. We have each other's backs, even after death," Timber said, earning a grumble of agreement from the other rabbits.

"When I was searching for Wind, I found him fighting off three colony filth at the border. He shows great promise," Hemlock boasted.

Wind glanced at him, alarmed. *That's hardly the truth!* He hadn't fought them off, he had been chased off, and Chill had barely even touched him. But he didn't say anything, seeing the advantage to the exaggerated version of the fight.

"Really?" Timber started to circle him menacingly, occasionally nudging him or brushing against him in hopes of intimidating him, but Wind stood his ground. He forced himself to look ahead, remaining relaxed.

Eventually, Timber gave up and stopped in front of him, looking thwarted.

"Timber, remember when I told you about a kit killing Crimson? That was Wind," Hemlock informed Timber cautiously.

"I wish I could've been there to see it. Nothing really happens around here during the day." Timber blew out a breath and sat down, his expression wistful.

"You weren't there?" Wind tipped his head in surprise.

Timber gave him a long look. "Let's just say that I'm an exile among exiles. After Billy was killed, Silver and I competed viciously for his place. After she won, I decided it was best for me to go. I had gotten word that after our last squabble—the one in which I lost my eye—she planned to kill me the next morning. I remembered that Hemlock and I had worked together in Billy's group before I sought leadership, and I went to him for help.

"Hemlock, too, remembered our promises, and decided to bring me here. Before Billy became leader, we all used to meet here. But then, after he became leader, we all started meeting in his den. This is a safe, secluded place where we can talk freely, and train freely."

"Then why is Stride keeping watch?"

"To make sure you weren't followed from the border. Anyway, I'm almost completely healed now, but I've been training to get my strength back up. All of us, or sometimes just a few of us, will occasionally go out at night to train."

"Which we do by hunting down rabbits from the main exile group," Wind finished. "That was you, all of you? Even the worst back at camp are afraid to wit's end to go out at night because that's when a lot of rabbits go missing."

"That's the advantage of being in this group: safety in the dark. Would you like to train with us tonight?" Timber offered, eyes shining in the gloom.

I could be safe. Completely safe. And this seems like a good opportunity to gain success. "Sure. But do you rabbits sleep here? Is this a separate camp?"

"I sleep here, and Hemlock sometimes does too, but you need to stay in the main camp so that there's no lingering suspicion that this group is still alive. And to my understanding, you're second in command. That's a direct route to leadership. Once you have leadership, you can welcome me back into the exiles. Now let's go train," Timber said gruffly, before heading toward where Water had entered the camp with Hemlock. It was by then dark enough that his paws were just a dim outline against the earth. He strained to see what was ahead of them, but between the black blanket of night, and Timber's shoulders blocking his view, it was nearly impossible.

Despite his efforts to reassure himself, Wind felt uneasy. *What would Water say if he knew I was doing this?* Then he shook his head bitterly. *As if he could spare a single thought that it is not about his precious Root.*

The night was mostly silent, seeing that most exiles knew better than to travel alone at night. He glanced around in a vain attempt to get an idea of their location.

"There!" Timber whispered sharply, motioning a paw toward where a silver shadow wandered through the trees. The rabbit appeared to be a female, with many scars that stood out against her fur. Suddenly, the rabbit pricked her ears, and turned sharply to look at where they hid. In a moment, he recognized her.

Silver!

Wind felt a swell of panic, and his oath of loyalty to her came rushing back. He couldn't betray that. Silver deserved his loyalty more than this small, hopeless band of rogues. *What was I thinking?*

"Silver, watch out!" he called, his cry piercing the silence. Then, his paws almost seeming to belong to some other creature, he turned sharply on Hemlock and tackled the white rabbit.

Silver sprang into action, her eyes locking on the familiar face of Timber. "Aargh! I knew I should've killed you when I had the chance!" She leapt on him and he fell backward, still in shock of Wind's betrayal. Silver set a flurry of slashes at Timber's face.

Hemlock writhed underneath him, causing Wind to realize just how powerful the burly exile was. "What do you think you're doing? You belong to us!" Hemlock growled angrily.

"I made no oath," Wind retorted, rolling over while gripping Hemlock's shoulders. "You assumed as much, and said you wanted for me to just try this out! I have previous commitments."

Hemlock snarled in frustration. "Of course! A kit being second-in-command, no way! She made you make her a deal."

"She didn't have to." Wind grunted as he felt the weight of Buzzard on his back, and he rolled again. Buzzard was now being crushed underneath him, while he kicked both rear legs into Hemlock's exposed stomach.

Silver was finishing off Timber, but repeatedly had to pause to fight off Stride, giving Timber enough time to recover some ground and aid Stride. It was an endless, desperate cycle, and she was refusing to call to Wind for help, but Wind had his own opponents to deal with.

Growling, Wind viciously sliced Buzzard across the eyes, blinding his enemy. He slammed Hemlock against a tree, and the white rabbit fell back to the ground, unconscious. He shook out his fur before leaping at Stride. It was easy to drive off the gray-furred rabbit, who already was limping from a nasty shoulder wound.

Silver stood panting, head lowered from the exhaustion of the ambush.

"Silver?"

"What?" Her voice was an angry snarl.

"Are you injured?"

"Of course I'm injured. We were outnumbered."

He felt partly relieved that she hadn't seemed to notice that he had been prowling with the group that had attacked her. As far as she was concerned, he had just happened to be out at night, and had spotted them sneaking up on her.

"I was out exploring. I discovered their camp," he lied.

"What? Where?" She looked about in interest. "We must attack it and get rid of them at once."

"You're injured, and it's the middle of the night. We will attack when you are well again."

She glared at him. "That had better be a suggestion, for your sake."

He stood firm. "I am forcing you to see logic in the state that you are in. You must rest, and I will keep the other exiles in their place. I will tell them not that you are injured, but that you are planning."

"And when they ask what for?"

"I'll claw them. They shouldn't be much more curious after that."

Silver was nodding in agreement. "See to it then. Also, make sure my route to my den is secure and deserted. Is that clear?"

"Yes." He felt irritated, knowing full well what Silver was doing. She was trying to affirm her authority by giving him extra orders, and making sure he understood exactly what she wanted, but he didn't argue, instead stalking ahead to check the path to the camp.

CHAPTER ELEVEN

Muscles tensed. Water leapt at Light, arcing to the side right before impact, and then rammed his shoulder into his instructor's side with careful precision. Light stumbled for a moment, then turned on him and they circled each other, eyes sharp with anticipation of who would have to make the next move.

But then Light stopped, glancing up at the sun. "I think that's all we'll do for today. This has been another good session, and you are improving greatly. Now go, get something to eat, and then rest up. We'll start from here first thing tomorrow morning, so be ready."

Water was disappointed, feeling as if they were just getting started. He wanted to continue, to practice until it was too dark to see his own paws, but he knew Light was right to stop for the day. Mainly, he wanted to get caught up in training so as not to think about Chill's request to Deerface. *Light understands me. I can talk openly to him because we share a common goal.*

"Hold on a minute, Light." They both jumped as Deerface padded from the nearby tunnel entrance and glanced at both of them. "I was hoping to stop and watch for a minute, but I guess I'm a little late for that. Do you mind practicing a little longer?"

Light eyed Deerface quizzically. "The leaders never watch training sessions, and Water is tired."

"I don't mind. I could train until sunrise. Light gives me so many great tips to save energy while fighting," Water said eagerly. *Deerface needs to see for himself that Light is a good rabbit and that he's on our side.*

Deerface looked satisfied, sitting down with a nod for them to proceed. "Go on. Continue as you would as if I wasn't here."

Light nodded and faced Water again. "Let's try the hind paw advance, all right? I want you to try to get as close to me as you can without your front paws touching the ground. Go!"

Water reared up, staggering awkwardly toward Light, who was ducking low to knock him over. Water narrowed his eyes and swept downward, and Light retreated to avoid the slashes raining down on him. But then he reared back up and they struck at each other over and over, blocking, aiming, and taking blows constantly. It was a grueling process, a battle of endurance: who would falter first?

Too easy, Water thought. *My forearms are stronger than his, my hind legs more accustomed to this type of fight.*

Panting, Light finally gave in, returning to all four paws on the ground. "Excellent work, Water. Now, how could that help in a real battle?"

"If my front paw or shoulder got injured, or if I need height on my opponent," he answered promptly.

"Good. What if one of your hind legs was wounded?"

"I'd tuck it under me so that they couldn't target me where I'm already weak."

Deerface stepped forward again. "That's a common tactic for exiles. They'll see a healing injury and try to reopen it. That takes less effort. By hiding injuries you can avoid fatal errors."

"And you can also fluff out your fur by giving it a shake before a fight. This way you'll make yourself appear bigger and intimidate your enemy, and hide any injuries you might already have, though you shouldn't have to fight if you're already injured," Light added rapidly, shooting a glare at Deerface for interrupting.

Deerface returned it coldly. "Yes, an intimidated enemy is one already half beaten."

Water glanced from one to the other in confusion.

Light was silent, unwilling to provoke their leader.

Water shuffled his paws awkwardly. "So, how is Nettle doing as a Messenger?" he asked to break the prolonged silence.

Deerface slowly turned his head to look at Water. "I'm sure he's getting on well enough. Scale is a good instructor."

"Haven't you gone to check on his training, as well? Surely the well-being of *all* of our brothers concern you, not only as a leader, but as a sibling?"

"Why do I feel that you aren't just talking about Nettle?" Deerface then froze, his gaze becoming sharper. "Did Chill speak to you?"

Water growled. "He didn't have to! I took matters into my own paws."

Deerface gave Water a long, appraising look, then his eyes narrowed.

"You eavesdropped on our meeting, didn't you?" Deerface snarled quietly.

Water lifted his chin defiantly.

"I knew that Chill would lie about what went on at the border, that he was wanting to pin suspicion on me. I also knew that he would never say those things to my face."

"Chill is—" Deerface suddenly sighed. "He is sick. He doesn't understand anything happening to him right now. His head is stuck in the past." Deerface shook his head sadly. "His statements cannot be trusted right now, seeing as he has lied so much. Every moment he is reliving his regrets and has turned his anguish against us."

"So does that mean I can't trust you? You are both obviously regretting past decisions, but I have found a way past that. I fix things, nurture them, instead of thinking about how I could have prevented them."

Deerface fixed his eyes at a point in the distance, his expression unreadable.

"So you found out about your brother." Deerface sighed wearily. "I knew this day would come. But I didn't send Wind away because Jo had a claim to him, or because I thought he was evil."

"But why then? He wants to come home so badly, but he can't because he has killed to survive. He would have been great with us."

"It's complicated, Water. There was a prophecy about you two. One that gave me great cause for concern. Light, leave us please," Deerface ordered swiftly, and Light obeyed immediately.

Deerface looked around before going on. "The prophecy said that 'Wind and Water together will destroy us all.' Their mixture is dangerous. I knew that it was referring to you and your brother. I hated to tear you apart, but I did it to protect everyone. To keep us all safe."

"Well, your prophecy was wrong. And I can prove it. Wind and I have done no rabbit any harm in our meetings. We relate to each other. After all, it was *your* lie and *your* decision to separate us that drove us together."

Deerface stared at him in wide-eyed horror. "Meetings? That cannot continue. I forbid it!"

"You can't do that! He's all alone there in a pack of killers. I'm the only good thing that's ever happened to him, the only thing keeping him from becoming a savage like his campmates. Nothing will separate us, we promised each other that!"

"You have responsibilities here. You cannot meet with an exile and still be completely loyal to us. If you want to meet Wind, then join him. But think very carefully before you do. Once you join your brother, there is no coming back from that."

"I don't know what future the colony offers me. Sometimes I don't think I have a future at all. I'm lost." Helplessness formed a suffocating lump in Water's throat.

"No future? You have the makings of a leader. If you cut ties with Wind for good, then I promise you a spot beside me as soon as you finish your training. You cannot live two lives, Water, if the entire colony is depending on you to be loyal to them first, to protect them from the exiles, including Wind."

Leader... That's all I've ever wanted. But to sacrifice Wind for my personal gain? That's a low, cruel blow. But then, he always wanted me to be a leader. He's encouraged and helped me toward it. Maybe this would be better for both of us. If he gets caught meeting me, he'll be killed. I'm just as much a danger to him as he is to himself.

"Can I have some time to think?" he asked Deerface desperately.

"To think about what?" Deerface eyed him cautiously. "Becoming a leader, or staying with us at all? Are you actually thinking about leaving us for the life of an exile? Root would be devastated, and she'll end up just like Chill because of it. A would-be mate leaving her for the exiles."

"No, I want to stay with the colony, and I do want to be a leader. I want it more than you can possibly imagine. But I can't just suddenly abandon Wind again. The first time we were just kits. But now I'm responsible for my own actions. I need to slowly let him go, for both our sakes." Water averted his eyes from Deerface's, studying the ground with a terribly hollow feeling in his chest.

"All right, I understand. But finish this before your training is through. When are you next meeting him?" Deerface's voice was grim.

"Tonight."

CHAPTER TWELVE

Wind sprinted up the slope, puffing for breath as he skidded to a stop in front of Water. He felt relief and excitement to see his brother, but it faltered at the deeply troubled and guilty look on Water's face.

"Hey, what happened?" he asked lightly, sitting down beside Water under the rocky overhang. Had someone hurt him? The thought made Wind growl.

"Deerface offered me the rank of leader once I complete my training," Water spoke quietly.

Wind was confused. "That's great! It's what you've always *wanted.* So why do you look so sad?" he asked hesitantly.

Water finally looked at him, eyes searching his. "If I accept this, it means that I'll have so many more responsibilities, serious ones. I'll be constantly busy. I'll be—"

"Unable to meet me," Wind finished for him, his shoulders stiffening. "We *promised* that nothing would *ever* separate us, not where we live or what we say and do."

"I know we did, Wind, but this opportunity is *real*."

"So you're saying that this, what we have here, what we've shared as brothers, is not real? Or that it is less real? What, you don't have time for me anymore?" A kernel of an idea formed in his mind. "Why not join me? We can protect each other, and you can be a leader there, except that you'll have more *freedom*. Please, come with me. It isn't so bad there. I've managed so far, haven't I?"

"Because you've had to *kill*, Wind. I don't know if I could do that. And it isn't just me. My family, my friends. I can't just abandon them. And I can't just walk away from Root. I *love* her. I'm sorry, but I can't live like that," Water declared, shaking his head sadly.

"Yet you and the other colony filth expect for *me* to. It's okay as long as it's some other rabbit that's suffering, I guess," Wind said bitterly, refusing to meet Water's gaze.

"No, you've got it all wrong. I'm accepting this rank *because* I don't want other rabbits to suffer. Why can't you just be happy for me?"

"Because *you* are my happiness, Water, but I don't have enough happiness to go around."

"You would if you didn't keep it to yourself. This is *my* decision, and it *has* been made. You can accept that and feel happy for me, or you can be bitter about it, but that's your choice. We'll still see each other around the border. This doesn't have to be goodbye," Water reasoned.

"No, it's not the same. If you want to choose mangy colony filth instead of your own brother, the only one who you could ever really talk to, then I don't want to see you, and I certainly don't want to talk to you. Don't you ever ask me for any favors. If you do this to me, you won't live very long to regret it."

Water leapt to his paws and faced him. "Are you *threatening* me?"

"Don't doubt it. Next time I see you, I'll kill you."

"Then get off my land, exile," Water spat.

Feeling a sharp pain in his heart, a mixture of anger and sorrow, Wind glared at Water for a few more moments and then turned away, head down. He made for the border, but before he reached it, he saw a pair of glowing green eyes in the undergrowth.

"Come out, I know you're in there," he growled.

To his amazement, Silver padded out and stood her ground, glaring at him. "What do you think you are doing here, meeting and talking with that colony filth?" she demanded.

"That was Water, my littermate. I thought he understood and cared about me, but I was wrong. He cares more about himself and what he wants." Wind padded dejectedly past her.

Silver kept pace. "What were you expecting from a colony rabbit?"

He stopped and looked her in the eye. "I wanted him to join us. At first it was just for strength, and because he's my littermate, but now it's because it would shove it in Deerface's face that he has no power over me. But Deerface got to Water first."

"Offered him leader?" Silver sat down and gazed steadily at him. "You know, when Billy was trying to get Deerface to join the exiles, Runt played the same trick on him."

"Deerface!" he spat venomously. "He's to blame for this! If he hadn't tempted Water like that, then Water would be here with us, where he belongs. If I so much as catch a whiff of his scent, he's dead, same for any of my kin from across the border. I'll lure them here if I have to."

Silver thought for a moment, glancing upward. "That might not be a bad idea. If we lure the leaders here and kill them, then their followers will be defenseless and will fear us. All we have to do is stage a trap and ambush."

"Leave it to me." Wind swept aside some leaves to reveal a barren patch of dirt. He traced lines in it as he spoke, the idea piecing itself together in his mind as he went. "Here's how we can do it. This is the tree line, and this is where we will crouch. On either side of us will be a half-circle of our best fighters, ready to surround the leaders." He made a long straight line, with two dots on one side, and four on the other. He etched a half-circle around the two dots, then looked up at Silver.

She gazed down at his work, still thinking, but looking impressed. "How will we get all four of them out here?" she murmured. Then Silver straightened up, eyes shining. "I've got it! Chill sits at the border all the time, so you could approach him and say that you want the colony to take you back. Try to convince him as sincerely as you can that you don't want the life of an exile. Tell him that you want to discuss this with all four leaders at the border because you don't want to cause a problem by just showing up in their tunnels. The rest of us will hide some way off until we hear them arrive, and then we'll all circle around to trap them."

"Brilliant!" Wind told her. "When should this take place?"

"Three days' time, in the morning. We must prepare our rabbits, teach them extra and make sure they all have the procedures down. Now let's get back to camp."

CHAPTER THIRTEEN

Water felt uneasy as he thought about the glare Wind had given him before padding away into the trees. He let out a long breath before sinking to the ground.

What have I done? Wind hates my guts. But he wasn't worried about himself or his abilities to fight Wind off. *He could target that rage against Root. Oh, no, what have I done?*

He rested his head on his paws and gazed out over the landscape. *On our first meeting, Wind was so captivated by the moorland. He gave me that, and I made it so that he could never feel the wind again.*

Water's vision started to blur, until his eyes shut, and he fell asleep.

****

"You! I'll kill you!" Wind looked down at him with a snarl of hate, perched atop a towering boulder.

He suddenly dove downward, claws outstretched, as if he were a bird about to snatch up its prey with powerful talons. Wind hit him, and they both skidded several paces. His brother pinned him down against the turf that was slick with blood.

Suddenly, Wind's cruel, sharp blue eyes transformed to brown, his face becoming wider. His fur drifted away and was rapidly replaced with thick, brown and white fur.

Chill?

"I'll kill you! Why didn't you just keep meeting your brother? That would have made every rabbit happier! I didn't want to have to do this, but you left me no choice." Chill raised one wide paw over Water's neck and brought it down forcefully.

* * *

Water woke with a gasp, his throat aching as if two heavy paws had reached through the nightmare and really choked him. He rolled over and sat up, uneasy with the clinging memories of his dream.

Chill wanted to be leader, and I took it instead. He understood now. *Well, he's never going to steal it from me.*

Shakily, he stood and trotted toward the tunnels. Deerface needed to know that he had kept his word.

On his way to the ceremonial room, he began to pass by his den, but was stopped by a quiet whisper.

"Water? Where were you?" Root padded out, blinking sleep from her eyes. She peered closer at him. "My, you look like a mess. Tell me, did you fall in the stream, or roll in some dirt?"

"No, and *thanks*," he huffed, sparked by her affectionate humor. "I slept on the moorland."

"Another meeting with Wind." She looked disappointed. "So, where are you heading?"

"Ceremonial Cavern. I need to speak with Deerface. Can I explain on the way?" he asked, motioning for her to join him.

"You may," Root replied, her eyes narrowing.

They walked for a while in silence, side by side. "Well, Deerface offered to make me a leader with him," he announced.

"That's great. Were you just on your way to tell him you accept, then?"

"I've already accepted. But he told me I had to completely break things off with Wind if I did," Water explained quietly, shame washing over him.

"I'm so sorry, Water." She sounded sincere. "I know how much he meant to you. I'll go with you to tell the leaders. You don't need to be alone."

He gave her a grateful glance, and they continued on in silence.

The ceremonial room was dimly lit by the frosty white moonlight streaming in from the tiny hole in the roof. To his surprise, Deerface was already there, sitting expectantly on the raised section of the floor. He stood as they entered.

"I thought you might stop by here tonight," Deerface greeted them.

"It's done. Wind wants to tear my head off now."

"Look, you may not see this now, but later on you will realize that this is for the best," Deerface tried to explain.

"Yeah, that's saying that a 'later' is in my future. Wind promised to *kill* me."

“He’ll get over it.”

“Tell me.” Water took a slow step toward Deerface, eyes watchful. “Why did you do it? Why couldn’t you have just kept my littermate here for a little bit longer instead of turning him into this, a killer? He has feelings, wants, he has good in him. I know he does. He has the capacity to love and improve. We could have prevented this.”

Deerface leaned toward him, looking deeply into the younger rabbit’s eyes. “Oh Water, do you think I haven’t asked myself that same question a thousand times over? I hate myself for sending that poor kit away, but I had to weigh the danger foretold in the prophecy. He could have destroyed us all.”

“*Could have?* Because now that’s exactly what he wants to do. What might he have done if you had given him a chance? You know what? I’m glad that you’re recruiting a new rabbit as leader, because I know I would never make a mistake like the one you made.” Water turned sharply and stalked out, fuming.

"Water, wait!" Deerface called, but he ignored him.

If he wants to ruin another rabbit's life before it has even begun, then he needs help more than Chill.

CHAPTER FOURTEEN

Wind looked at each exile in turn, a line of broad-shouldered, scarred, deadly killers over which he ruled and commanded. The day's sunlight was fading.

Silver seemed satisfied with his choices. "They will do."

"I've already made sure each of them knows the plan perfectly and shored up on their fighting skills. Tomorrow morning, they will make sure our plan is executed, quite literally."

"Good. And what about you? Do you know what to say, forward and backward?" she asked in an icy growl.

"Absolutely," he replied instantly.

Silver nodded. "Then get out of my sight, all of you! Rest tonight, tomorrow fight."

Wind made his way to his den in the bramble bush, his thoughts dark and brooding. After a while, his mind finally calmed, and he slept.

* * *

Wind was walking through the woods, his light gray paws falling softly on the leaf-litter. He looked about himself cautiously, scanning every inch of undergrowth. The faint breeze changed, carrying to him the scent of other exiles. He tensed, ready for a fight.

Suddenly, the forest erupted with noise, rabbits closing in on him from all angles, too many to count. They snarled as they leapt at him, and he snarled back, lashing out with all four paws, kicking and sweeping his legs about.

He was way outnumbered but refused to cower. "You want a fight? I won't make this easy!"

They flooded in, tackling him, biting and clawing viciously. He gave one last growl before falling…

* * *

Wind jerked awake, looking around his den suspiciously. He jumped as Silver stuck her head in.

"Get up, we're leaving now," she ordered abruptly before retreating.

He groomed himself hastily and joined her out in the main camp, where their followers were lined up, ready to go.

Without a word, Wind ran ahead, making a dash straight to the border where Chill mourned. Sure enough, his older brother was there, sitting with head down, shoulders hunched.

"What do you want?" Chill grumbled without looking up.

"Please," he said, mustering as much desperation as he could into his words. "I need to speak with the colony leaders. I-I can't live with the exiles anymore, and I'm willing to tell them everything I know if they'll just take me back in, correct their mistake, and let me correct mine. Please."

Chill raised his head, looking surprised. "Come with me, and I'll take you to them."

"I-I can't. I don't want to cause trouble if the colony rabbits see me in their tunnels. I need to talk to them here, please. Along with Water. I want to apologize to him, as well. Something happened. The exiles tried to kill me! Please, Chill, do this for me."

"All right, all right, just wait here." Chill turned to go.

"Wait! I need to make peace with *all* of them, including Water!" He made sure Chill understood.

Chill twitched his ears toward Wind as a signal that he had heard, and disappeared across the moorland.

Wind turned and nodded into the trees, hoping that Silver would see.

Then he sat absolutely still, his face a stony mask, and waited for Chill to return.

CHAPTER FIFTEEN

Water, Root, and Cedar hurried along the passage to the Ceremonial Cavern behind Light and Fern. Their instructors were agitated at the interruption to their combined training session, but Chill had seemed urgent.

"What could they want with us?" Cedar asked in a whisper. Then his eyes gleamed. "Maybe we're about to finish our training!"

"But Boulder isn't here," Root reasoned.

"Maybe they didn't think he was ready yet." Cedar sounded unbothered.

"Dens graduate together. They wouldn't leave him behind." Root looked perplexed.

Water was silent, still thinking. He was still lost in thought when the leaders arrived.

Deerface and Runt were pacing, side by side, while Spatula supported Stewie off to one end of the room. They each wore identical expressions of grim worry.

"He's here. Let's go." Deerface made a start for the exit.

"What's going on?" Water refused to follow.

Deerface halted. "Wind wants to speak to us about coming back into the colony, and he wants you there."

"He said he'd kill me the next time he saw me. That was three days ago. I don't trust him."

"I said, let's *go*. I want to hear him out," Deerface argued, something Water couldn't quite place poorly hidden in his eyes.

"Then at least let my denmates and their instructors go, just in case we need backup."

"Fine." Deerface looked unhappy with his objection but held his head high. "But I'm telling you now that it will not be necessary. Wind came to make peace."

"You thought the same of Darkside right before he attacked you in the Great Ambush," Water shot back.

Deerface glared wordlessly at him before giving them all the signal to head out. Water returned it defiantly as he filed past his leader. *He knows that he'll have to get used to this, me being able to argue with him without a rank between us to silence me.*

Water felt apprehensive. *I know how angry Wind was. He wouldn't just turn around and try to make peace. He's planning some kind of treachery.*

They emerged onto the moorland, and Water blinked rapidly to get used to the harsh sunlight. Deerface took the lead beside Runt, marching commandingly toward the border. As they went, Water's anxiety grew, along with his suspicion.

The trees loomed overhead. Wind was waiting silently for them, but he arose as they came closer.

Water peered closely at him, but Wind's face was guarded. That wasn't the face of a rabbit who wanted to reconcile.

"Thank you for coming, Deerface." Wind dipped his head respectfully. "I wanted to ask for a place in the colony. Please, do that for me. I want to end this between us."

Water pushed forward roughly and shoved his face in his littermate's. "You promised to kill me next time you saw me. And now you expect me to believe you've had a miraculous change of heart? I won't fall for your tricks, Wind."

"Yet, you still came here." Silver padded out to stand beside Wind, and the shadows suddenly came alive as teems of burly exiles seethed forward and surrounded them, cutting off any escapes.

The other leaders growled, quickly forming a defensive circle with their backs to each other. Water, his denmates, and their instructors joined them.

"Runt, this is just like with Claw!" Spatula whispered sharply to her old comrade. "We must use the same strategy."

"How could you do this?" Chill faced Silver in disbelief.

She looked away. "I'm not who I used to be."

Wind snarled. "Enough of this! It's time to die!"

"Wait!" Cedar looked Wind daringly in the eye. "Water warned all of us that you would try something like this. That is why we have all of our strongest Patrollers waiting just over the hill to come to our aid."

"You're bluffing!" an exile called.

"We aren't stupid!"

"Silence!" Silver ordered. "They are just stalling. There is no help for them."

"Attack us, then. But just remember the last time you tried to ambush us—and what you lost. *This* time, we'll make sure to wipe you all out completely," Stewie growled darkly.

"Rock, Dicer, Viper, and Moth, go up and check it out," Wind ordered.

"No, hold the formation!" Silver contradicted him.

The exiles glanced around in confusion. The four Wind had ordered to scout tried to break away to obey, but others tackled them. The exiles fell into a fit of frustration and uncertainty, while the colony rabbits watched.

"No, *they* are the enemy! Attack!" Silver screeched, leaping at Chill with claws at the ready.

Wind lunged for Deerface, while Light, Fern, and Cedar defended themselves against four huge male exiles.

"Root, go fetch as many Patrollers, as many rabbits as you see. Send them here!" Water called before being knocked off his paws by two exiles. He caught a glimpse of her spinning around and slipping past several exiles before making for the tunnels.

Water wriggled away before rearing up on his hind legs as Light had recently taught him, slashing down at his attackers, who had been joined by two others. They crowded him, slicing and biting and clawing in an attempt to bring him down.

Oh, no, he thought in despair. *If I fall over, they'll pounce on me, and I won't be able to get up again. It'll be over.* With more desperation, Water clawed back at the relentless exiles, but they kept ducking back. Each time one stepped out of range, he was replaced by another, all taking turns slashing at him. Water felt himself weakening with each blow, his legs quaking.

But then his assailants screeched in terror as a swarm of colony rabbits surged toward them like a wave, pushing the fight into the trees so that healers could tend to the wounded on the moorland.

Relieved beyond comprehension, Water let himself fall to the ground, his blood pooling around him. He only lay there, drifting between awareness and unconsciousness. The sounds of intense battle carried faintly to his ears, which were full with the thump of his heart in his chest.

Is it slowing, or am I just imagining it? He dragged his head to one side so that he could see the great gash in his side. *So much blood… Is it all mine? No, not anymore. It belongs to the ground now.*

His vision faltered, and Water groaned before a blackness swept over him.

CHAPTER SIXTEEN

Wind growled in frustration, glimpsing the colony reinforcements from the corner of his eye as he fought Deerface.

He is the reason for my suffering! I will not rest until he is dead.

Wind ducked a slash, then hunched one shoulder and barreled into the rival leader, who caught him. They locked dangerously, clawing frantically at each other. Wind managed to strike out with a hind leg, but Deerface curved his body to avoid anything worse than a shallow cut.

"Exiles, back to camp!" Silver ordered, fleeing with several others on her tail. Wind shoved Deerface away reluctantly. The last thing he wanted was to be surrounded with no help.

He turned tail and sprinted for the forest, flinching from his seeping injuries. Wind looked back over his shoulder as he ran.

Deerface stood with paws splayed, shoulders hunched as he panted from exhaustion. Runt and Spatula joined him, glaring after Wind.

They may have won this battle, but the war has just begun. Sleep well, colony scum, because the next time you dare to close your eyes, it will be in death…

CHAPTER SEVENTEEN

Water's blood-crusted eyes flickered open painfully, and he hacked up dirt, feeling as if he was rooted to the ground, forever stuck in that horrible place.

The battlefield was barren, and not even the terrible screeches of fighting pierced the air. Everything was still, frozen, and utterly deserted.

Where is everyone? Was it all a dream? Have I just awoken from a night spent on the moorland, returning from a meeting with Wind? Water tried to sit up and gasped, the staggering agony of his wounds returning as he emerged from his numbed state. This was no dream.

Did the exiles win? Is that why no one has found me? Alarmed, Water propped himself up on his forelegs, clawing at the tough grass to drag himself forward. He made slow progress, eventually testing out his uninjured side. It buckled briefly, but soon he was hopping along slowly.

A tunnel entrance yawned darkly before him, and Water hobbled into it, using the wall to steady himself. *I must be close to the Collectors' section. No one will be here at this time of day. They'll all be out working. It's all come down to me—I've got to get to the Ceremonial Cavern. I-I can't make it that far. I need to rest.*

Water found a shallow niche in the passage, most likely chipped out by a falsely started tunnel, and slumped over, the throbbing gash in his side facing upward. He panted quietly, until his head lolled in sleep.

* * *

Water entered the Ceremonial Cavern. He looked around, but his head snapped toward a shuffling sound from the leader's den. He watched, fear fluttering in his chest, as Wind emerged, yawning as if he had just woken up. But something was different. Wind looked, what, older? *Much older.*

"What do you think you are doing? This is a sacred room!" he snarled in bewilderment.

Wind looked surprised to see him standing there. "Who are you?"

"What do you mean, who am I? Who are you, acting as if you own this place? You murderous, flea-ridden exile! Get out of here!"

Wind looked disturbed. "I must be dreaming. Are you my spirit-rabbit?"

"What? *I'm your littermate, Wind. You swore to kill me!"*

"No, I would never kill. I belong here, a leader beside Deerface and Spatula. We are the Three. My brother Water was an exile."

"What do you mean, was *an exile?" Water was scared of the answer.*

Wind dropped his head. "We had to kill him, even if he took Runt and Stewie with him. He was out of control. But it was necessary." A steely glint entered Wind's eyes. "The remaining exiles agreed to a peace settlement after he died, for they hated him for the tyrant that he was."

"No, you are the exile! You and Silver ambushed us at the border. You declared war on us!"

"There is no war. There is peace. My rabbits are content."

* * *

Water gasped, head pounding. He clawed himself out of the niche in the tunnel, and glanced around, trying to get his bearings. He felt a sense of urgency. Clenching his jaw in response to the fiery pain, he hurried to the Ceremonial Cavern, stumbling and falling almost constantly on his way.

Water rounded a corner and tripped on a jutting rock, landing on his face. He shook the pain, cursing crossly, before getting back to his paws and moving on once more.

Suddenly he burst into the room, fighting for breath. Spatula sat in the entrance to the tunnel that led to her den, head down. She looked up in bewilderment as Water heaved himself the last few steps and crumpled to the floor just before the dais.

"*Water?*" Spatula said in pure shock. "But, *how*? You never returned from the ambush. We all thought you were *dead!* Every rabbit assumed that you had been killed across the border, after we were driving the exiles back into the trees, and that they had dumped your body into the stream! You were being completely *swarmed* by them."

"Where are the others?" he gasped, his fear increasing.

"They are mourning you and Stewie. I stayed in case any rabbit showed up in need of something. Are you all right? I can barely recognize you under all of that blood!" Spatula hurried over and started sniffing him, looking concerned to see his fur ruffled and laced with cuts, some of which still trickled blood.

"My side…" He angled his ears at the wound, shivering from the shooting torment.

"Oh, great rabbit!" Spatula exclaimed in dismay. "Wait here while I go fetch supplies and a couple of other Healers."

Well, that's easy enough, seeing as I can't do much more than wait. He felt a piercing sadness, grief. *Stewie, dead! This is my fault. If I hadn't been so selfish by leaving Wind, he would never have attacked us…*

But you don't know that, a small voice in his head argued. *They would have attacked eventually. And Stewie hated fighting, no matter how skilled she was at it. Maybe it's better that she won't have to suffer what is to come. After all, a war has begun.*

What's the point in being so skilled, if all of the good rabbits are just killed?

CHAPTER EIGHTEEN

Wind marched over to Silver's den and halted abruptly in the entrance with his paws planted and chin raised. She looked up from cleaning the blood from her fur, eyes narrowed with hostility.

"Careful, Wind, before you say things that you will regret," she warned darkly.

"I already regret one thing I said a long time ago," he growled pointedly, referring to his oath.

"You cannot betray me now, Wind. This is a war, and we have no time for either that or your pettiness. Now, go get me a count of the survivors, and an accounting of the injured," she snapped curtly, turning away from him.

"I'm not finished!" he said sharply. "I no longer have confidence in your leadership. You set us up to lose out there, contradicting my orders like that. We needed to know if they actually had other rabbits in waiting so that we could decide if it was worth it to stay and fight."

Silver glared furiously at him. "I hold a higher rank than you, so that was *my* choice to make. They wanted to break our formation, and you gave them a golden opportunity to do so."

"No, we had *plenty* of rabbits so that they could never have escaped. We brought extra rabbits for that exact situation. Our followers clearly thought that scouting out their formation was the best choice, which is why they tried to obey me, until you caused a mess of confusion."

"*My* followers don't *get* a thought. The four that disobeyed me will be severely punished for costing us this victory. They knew better than to listen to you before me."

"They will not be punished in any way. If there is a rabbit at fault, that would be you, Silver. You weaken us."

She snarled low in her throat, slowly rising to her paws and advancing a step toward him. "I ruled effectively and efficiently before I made the mistake of promoting you. Now look at us! You becoming my second-in-command has not only weakened us, it has nearly destroyed us all! You and your little squabbles over your relationships with your colony brother, dragging the rest of us into it because you had your *feelings* hurt. Well, guess what? You let sentimentality cloud your judgement."

"At least I tried to *do* something instead of crumpling and whimpering in my den, never coming out but to humiliate or kill some rabbit who was ready to follow me to their death!" he spat as he advanced a step. "Rabbits must learn from trial and error, not trial and then being murdered for making a simple mistake. I should have just let Timber kill you—no, *I* should have just killed you. It is time for Billy's bloodline to come back into power. I have let you just go about humiliating us and bringing shame to what my father was trying to accomplish for far too long. It is time for me to finish his work before you completely demolish what is left of it."

"Are you *challenging* me?" Silver spat, astounded.

"Absolutely. You can either surrender leadership to me right this instant, or you can attempt to take me on in combat."

"I would sooner die than take orders from you, a senseless kit!" Silver reared up, her eyes blazing with more anger and hate than he had ever seen in the eyes of any rabbit.

They both exited the den, coming to stand in the center of the camp. Some rabbits looked up from grooming their slowly healing wounds, cautiously interested. A few were returning to camp, slowing to see the commotion.

"Exiles! I have been challenged by Wind for leadership, who in doing so has offered himself as an example of what can be expected for defying me. I will kill him, and you all will stand as witnesses!" Silver let her imposing, forest-green glare sweep around the clearing.

Several rabbits looked nervous both at the force of her wrath and the prospect of a fight to the death.

"Have you any last words?" Silver sneered at him.

Wind stood tall, forcing himself to remain calm and even, his gaze impassive. "Silver is no longer fit to lead you! I shall fulfill my father's legacy. His spirit favors me and lends me his strength. Now I am strong enough to take his place and am grateful to Silver for preparing it for me, but enough is enough. These are not last words, but the first words in a glorious new beginning!"

Wind turned to face Silver as the exiles formed a large, ragged circle around the edges of the clearing. All were struck with silence.

Hissing like a snake, Silver lunged at him in the first move, but Wind sidestepped, waiting for her to charge again. She skidded, digging her claws into the dirt to stop herself, before flipping back over, tensed.

Seeing that she wasn't about to try again, Wind flew at her, full force. Silver didn't move fast enough, and he rammed his head and shoulders forcefully into her stomach. Her eyes widened as she was thrown several strides away, writhing for breath.

Wasting no time, Wind raced at her, bowling her over as she tried to stand once more. He pinned Silver down, but she brought her legs up to her chest and kicked him in the face. Wind stumbled, and she managed to get away again. They circled each other cautiously.

"Come on, *fight* me! Stop trying to just hit me and retreat, you coward!" he bellowed.

Silver twitched her ears, but did not respond. It was clear now that she wouldn't stand a chance in close combat against him.

Giving up with trying to goad her into being reckless, Wind charged again. Silver flipped neatly over him, using his shoulders to propel herself upward. He twisted sharply, causing several of his smaller cuts to reopen, but curled his claws around her ankle and yanked her back down before she could finish the familiar move.

Silver gave a startled growl, unprepared. He put all his weight into pinning her down as he clawed her deeply down the length of her back, blood spilling from the gashes. Silver gritted her teeth, flailing desperately, now on the defensive.

Wind watched her writhe away, knowing that she was too badly injured now to move with any speed at all. He took his time to walk calmly over, stopping in front of her.

Silver looked up. "Go on, then, kill me. Prove that you are stronger. Once I am dead, they will then realize everything that I ever did for them, and they will *despise* you."

Wind shook his head. "I know I am stronger, Silver. I have always known that, and so have you. I need not kill you to prove that. I have already won. But physical strength is not the only thing that makes me better than you." He leaned forward, looking her right in the eye. "I have strength of mind. I am powerful enough that I can afford to show mercy. I do not need to kill the weak constantly for every rabbit to know that I am in charge."

"I will not serve you." She bared her teeth in abhorrence. "You might as well kill me here and now, or else I will cause you many problems in the future."

Wind straightened back up. "You are utterly alone, Silver. You are not worth my time."

Wind turned his back on her, trotting across the clearing as if he still had plenty of energy to spare, and flexed his muscles before springing to the top of the boulder in a powerful leap.

Unable to be anything but impressed by the view he now had, Wind waited silently for the exiles to gather below him, leaving Silver to slink away to the deeper shadows. They looked up at him expectantly, a respectful quiet settling over them.

"You've witnessed what has just occurred. Silver is defeated and disgraced, and I stand before you as your new leader. I shall choose my second-in-command," Wind announced, satisfied by the way his voice echoed commandingly throughout the camp. He let his eyes prod the crowd, noticing several of the stronger exiles sit up straighter, willing him to choose them for such a high rank, thirsting for the honor.

They know that whoever is chosen will never be picked on by any others, will do what they please, will be remembered throughout many generations…

Someone well-liked, who would be good at strategizing, and will be loyal…

"Ginger, step forward." Wind raised his chin as he called the name.

A sleek, bright orange rabbit wove her way to the very front and looked up at him with hazel eyes. The only family she had left, her sister, Lark, had been killed in the ambush. She had come with her littermate to the exiles when Lark had been accused of murder, and they had fled together before a proper trial could take place.

"Ginger, you of all rabbits should know how the weakness of our previous leader was dangerous, and your sister paid a high price for that foolishness. I hope that you will help me to push for a more organized, stronger group so that such tragedies are no more. Do you accept?"

"Yes, I accept." Ginger's voice rang out clearly and strong.

"Good. You are all dismissed." Wind leapt down, heading toward a burly, male rabbit named Blink.

Blink turned, attentive, as Wind reached him. "Yes, sir?"

"I want you in charge of fortifying the camp walls. No gaps for spies to see through, no places where a rabbit could sneak in or out. Use whatever you can find: branches, twigs, vines, anything you think will strengthen it. Pick several others to help you and tell them my orders. Is that clear?"

"Perfectly." Blink nodded swiftly, looking pleased to have been put in charge of something.

"Good, because I'm counting on you. If our camp is attacked, our enemies should not be able to break through. One main entrance and exit will be much easier to defend. Get to work."

Wind turned away and headed next to where Ginger sat, awaiting orders.

"All right, come with me." He pushed through the ferns to the clearing Silver had used to train him. He would sleep in the cave under the boulder from now on.

Wind angled his ears toward his old den within the bramble thicket. "That's yours from now on. The entrance is around the side. It's better if you sleep in this clearing so that I'm able to reach you at all times, and it should be safer than sleeping with the other exiles too."

Ginger nodded. "Shouldn't we reinforce the walls in this clearing, as well? There's a fallen tree over there that we could use the branches of to help. It's also crawling with vines."

"Good idea. I'll haul branches over, then, if you'll collect some thorn tendrils and vines to weave in." Wind made his way through the tall ferns and grass ringing the small clearing, reaching the fallen tree with ease.

Several branches had cracked off from the impact of hitting the ground, so he grabbed the largest one he could carry and retreated.

After a while of rather taciturn, yet diligent labor, Wind paused, panting with exertion.

"Go get a report from Blink about how the barrier construction is going," he ordered Ginger, who obeyed without a word.

Wind padded slowly over to his new den and settled down, lying halfway in and halfway out, his head reposed on his paws. He admired the work they had completed as he rested.

Suddenly, the huge, burly gray-and-white shape of a rabbit shouldered its way through a gap in the new wall, brown eyes looking back in disdain. "You really shouldn't doze off until this is impenetrable, you know. A rabbit my size should have more difficulty breaking in to kill all of you."

"How dare you just stroll in here, colony filth! This is *my* camp, and I will kill you to defend it!" Wind leapt to his paws and growled menacingly at the newcomer.

"Whoa, who says I wasn't just exiled? Or that I'm new to this island?" He looked Wind dead in the eyes, not bothering to get an idea of their surroundings.

"No rabbit is new to this island! It is too secluded, and don't tell me you swam across the ocean to get here, because I swear I'll rip you to pieces!" Wind growled in warning.

The rabbit looked amused. "Oh, I'm certainly not a stranger to this camp or this island, seeing as I helped to found the main colony. My name is Billy, no further introductions needed. I am here to help my son restore the exiles to their former glory, as you have expressed you are so eager to do."

Wind's jaw dropped. "But you're dead! Deerface killed you before I was even born."

Billy rolled his eyes. "I live on in spirit, as well as in you, my kit. Deerface did not kill me, his spirit-rabbit, Slate, did the honors." Billy started to circle him in the clearing, while Wind followed him carefully with his eyes. "My approbation for you and your accomplishments is very high, my son. Of all my kin, you were the one strong enough, smart enough, courageous enough to carry out my work."

"How are you here? Surely you would never be allowed anywhere near us?"

Billy sat down in front of him, paws tucked away under his chest. "Well, you see, since Slate broke many, many strict rules to kill me, the highest-ranking rabbits of all, the First Rabbits, as they are called, were enraged that a rabbit they had entrusted with so much power had abused it. As punishment to him, they gave me the ability to talk to the living rabbits as I would have had if I hadn't been killed so unjustly. After all, dying does give you quite a perspective. They can do anything imaginable, including imprisoning me, but they were merciful. They understand the benefits."

"Why didn't they just give you your life back, if they are so powerful?"

Billy turned his head, giving him a sidelong glance. "Because you and Water needed to be separated, and *you* needed to take my place." Billy took a breath, faced him again, and said, "If Deerface wasn't so weak, he would have killed me himself. If he wasn't so weak, he would have killed you and your brothers, and then there would be no 'doom-laden prophecy.'"

"Yes, but I'm going to throw Deerface's mercy back in his face, mark my words. He will regret sparing my life."

Billy made no comment. "Fix this wall," was all he growled before Wind blinked, and he was gone.

CHAPTER NINETEEN

Water winced as he tried once more to stand. Root and Spatula stood at the ready, arms outstretched in case this most recent attempt failed.

His wide, bluish-gray paws trembled at first, but after a few moments they became steadier. He reached out a forepaw and took a tentative step forward, delighted when it held his own weight. His side wound throbbed dully, but it was healing well, according to Spatula and Mud, the Head Healer.

"You're doing great, Water. Would you like to take a break before you get back at it again?" Spatula coaxed.

"No, no. It feels great to stand again. I can't quit now," Water replied as he concentrated on taking a few more steps.

Spatula looked uncertain. "Maybe you *should* rest again. Let us take care of you."

With a start, Water remembered when he and Root had seen Stewie and Deerface out on a walk one day, and what the brown-and-white-furred leader had implored to his much older, frail comrade: *"please, let us take care of you."*

He glanced at Root, feeling a wash of grief. She seemed to have the same reminiscence of that day, as well.

"Yeah, I think I'll take that rest," he gave in, downcast and nostalgic. *I wish Stewie was still here. She was a great storyteller and had a better mind for reality than most rabbits. She would have wanted to be remembered that way, she told me that herself.*

Water hobbled slowly back to his nearby nest and eased himself down into it, head and paws hanging over the shallow lip. Root touched her nose softly to his forehead, a quiet gesture of comfort.

"Wait," Water called quietly as she turned to rejoin Spatula. Root walked back to him and sat down, close enough that their fur brushed. "What are the leaders saying about the attack? Are we going to strike back?"

"They seem to want to decide when you are fully healed and able to help them make that decision," she replied, eyes shining.

"They're promoting me once I'm better?" he asked, thrilled.

"Yes." She pressed the top of her head to his chin affectionately. "Now, hurry up and get back to acting like your old self, or else I'll just have to finish training without a know-it-all whispering the answers to me."

Water snorted. "Remember that time when Fern caught me giving you the answer to that one strategy that helps you recover from being winded?"

"He was so angry!" Root nodded and laughed.

"Yeah, and telling him that you only needed to know how to do the move, and let your *instincts* tell you when to use it, didn't help at all!" Water nudged her as he recalled, distinctly picturing the strict old rabbit's searing, furious glare.

"Of course, den cleaning wasn't as bad since we had to do it together," Root admitted softly. She shook out her fur. "Now get to sleep, or else I'll get in trouble for keeping you awake."

"You never minded trouble, and I never minded talking to you." Water yawned, closing his eyes.

* * *

Water sat under his old meeting place with Wind, his confusion growing. How did I get here?

A light brown female rabbit with a huge mane of fur encircling her face boldly approached him, her brown eyes like endless pools of wisdom and intelligence. He had never seen this stranger before, but something about her seemed hauntingly familiar.

"Greetings, Water. My name is Bear. I believe you knew my litter sister, Stewie," she blinked, tipping her head to one side, as if waiting for him to speak.

Water let his head fall. "I know why you are here. It's because I'm to blame for Stewie's death. I will avenge her, you have my word."

Bear shook her head. "You are not at fault, Water. Yes, you will have to fight again, but not for the sake of my sister. I'm sure you would like to know that Wind is now the exile leader."

"He is? He betrayed his promise to Silver, then. A rabbit could only wonder what he will break next."

"Come with me." Bear gestured for him to follow

as she turned and headed for the border, continuing into the trees. Hostile territory.

"We cannot be here! The exiles may be a pack of criminals, but an agreement was settled. We shall keep our part, and keep out of their forest," Water explained urgently as he kept pace.

"When you are dead, the land belongs to no rabbit. We go where we please. You are dreaming, so you are not visible to their eyes." She led him straight to the exile camp, trotting through the entrance. Water noticed that several vines and branches looked new to the once tattered barrier.

Bear moved fluidly forward, passing a whisker's length from the rabbits who sat on watch noiselessly. He padded after her to a thin wall of ferns and tall grass, both of them pushing through.

Bear suddenly motioned for him to back up, retreating herself. "Your brother has company, the type that can see us. Let's circle around behind them, but try to remain silent. This rabbit is not one fond of surprise visitors."

They followed the thin wall around until Bear stopped, and together they peered through: a broad-shouldered, gray-and-white male rabbit sat beside Wind, both gazing out at the dense woodland over the protective perimeter as they spoke.

"Your brother is dead, Wind. It was Deerface's fault for forcing him to abandon you, but Water would never have agreed if his denmate Root was out of the picture. She stole him from you," the rabbit told him softly, insistently.

"And you're sure he's dead?"

"I wouldn't have made you suffer this news if he wasn't. I saw him walking with the dead, in our territory. Those colony filth just left him to die on the battlefield, left him to the vultures," the rabbit lied breezily.

No! *Water thought desperately.* This rabbit is lying! I'm not dead! You don't know him, so don't believe him!

"Wind, I know this is hard to hear for you, but keep in mind that I'm not only your spirit-rabbit, your destined protector, I am your father. I wanted to be here

for you, in the flesh, my son, but that chance was cruelly stolen from me by my own blood." Billy's eyes were wide and deceptively gentle as the words fell fluidly from his mouth.

"Deerface," Wind snarled hatefully. "How could he think that that was his choice to make? He stole everything from me! First you, then my normal life, and then he turned the rabbit I was closest to me against me, which forced me to have to attack and kill him." Pain flashed in Wind's striking blue eyes, but he quickly shook it off like he would a fly, and raised his head to lock eyes with Billy. "I will avenge you, father, as well as bring justice for my brother's death."

"Don't do this for me, Wind. Do this for you, for the rabbits that look to you as their leader. Take care of my group that I had prepared just for you," Billy growled gruffly, giving his son a proud nod.

"I will. But if you see Water again, will you tell him that all I ever wanted was to seek peace together with him?" Wind pleaded nervously. "I thought that if he became colony leader, and that if I became exile

leader, we could establish an alliance, and help each other. I have to kill Deerface for him. He said himself that Deerface was selfish for what he did and then kept from us. I never wanted for things to end this way."

"I'm sure he will understand when I tell him this," Billy said gently. "I will go now. Continue preparations."

Bear slid backward silently, retreating, and Water followed.

"Why is Billy saying these things? Why must Wind think I am dead?" he asked, perplexed.

Bear gazed grimly at him. "Billy and Eagle have tried several times since the ambush to kill you while you have been resting, but Stewie, Daisy, and I have fought them off every time. If Wind thinks you are dead, his hate for Deerface and the colony will fuel him. Grief and anger are focused into blame, which tells Wind where to strike out. But if he discovers you are actually alive, he will turn on Billy, focus that hate-driven blame on him instead."

Water nodded in understanding. "I would visit Wind in the waking world to show him I am alive, but I am injured too badly to travel more than a few steps. And how did Billy become Wind's spirit-rabbit, anyway?"

Bear looked away. "It was originally a rabbit named Shell, but Billy killed him in cold blood so that he could take his place."

"And no rabbit did anything to stop him? They just let Billy continue to whisper his lies into my brother's ears? Unbelievable!"

"Slate could have stopped him, as one of the foreseers for the First Rabbits, but since Slate had his abilities taken for killing Billy, the First Rabbits were practically blind to Billy's crime. The rest of us could not interfere, for the risk of suffering our own powers to be taken, which would leave whichever rabbit was under our watch utterly unprotected."

"Wait, so Deerface is just completely undefended? Billy could kill him at any time!"

"No, Slate had his extra-powerful abilities taken, but he can still protect Deerface with as much as I can protect you with. You must go now, but be careful.

Never be alone, for that is when Billy will strike you again. Always, when you are alone..." Bear looked more troubled. "And Water, tell Spatula that Stewie and I miss her dreadfully, just as Daisy says she misses Runt."

CHAPTER TWENTY

Wind grunted as he helped Blink and a few others to hoist up a new branch, setting it into the camp boundary. Once they had let it go, and it seemed steady, he took a few steps back, panting from their hard work, but satisfied by their progress in reinforcing the barrier.

"Unless they've learned to smash right through a tree, there's no way those colony filth will be getting through this!" Blink declared triumphantly.

Wind said nothing as he continued to inspect the newly fortified wall, and headed for the exit of the camp, where the two guards nodded to him as he passed. The sound of paw steps crunching over leaves made him look back to see that Ginger had followed him.

"Wind," she greeted him with a dip of her head. "Shouldn't we be planning our attack and defensive strategies soon? They could attack at any moment, but it would be wise of us to strike them first."

"What if no one strikes? What if the war is really over, but we are making up excuses to use our claws? We killed two of their leaders." Wind walked on, head low and weariness weighing like a stone in his chest.

"Where is this coming from?" She gaped at him in shock. "My sister was killed by them! They cannot get away with that."

"Your sister wouldn't want you to suffer the same fate. The cycle is endless. I just want to rest for once, you know? That ambush caused the death of my brother. As much as I'd like to, I can't just pretend that I stopped caring about him."

"You designed the ambush to ensure that Water would be there to die with his friends. So why are you moping about now? With all due respect, it was your fault that your and Silver's plan worked in some respects."

Wind stopped and turned his eyes on Ginger, struggling to decide how much he could trust her with, but he desperately needed to let out some of the thoughts crowding his mind. From what he had noticed, Ginger's sister had been her best friend, much like Water had been for Wind. *Maybe if I told her, she would understand?* "To be honest, I wanted Water to be there so that he could protect his leaders. His strength matched mine in all ways, maybe even exceeding it, which is why I had thought he could stop me. I was so *angry*, but I couldn't just back out of the plans that Silver and I had made."

"You wanted to lose?" Ginger was quieter. "Wind, how do you even know that he is dead? You haven't been out of camp at all since the battle. He could still be alive."

"No, my father has spoken with me many times. He told me that Water was killed in the fight."

"When Billy was alive, he also said that Jo was being held hostage by the colony rabbits to be a liability to him, but we all knew that he was having secret meetings with her. He said that as he was bleeding out, his father made him promise to kill Runt, but that was also disproved when Runt told us all about how Claw said that he never wanted for Billy to be like him. I didn't believe our campmates when they told me that Lark was dead, so I went to see her body for myself, and found that it was true."

"What are you saying I should do, then?"

"*Visit* him. The colony rabbits abstain from killing at all times, so you needn't worry."

"If he really is dead, then they'll lose their morals instantly and kill me on sight. This is a risk we cannot afford to take."

"On the contrary, Wind, this is a risk we must take. If we do not, the war will take a nasty turn."

CHAPTER TWENTY-ONE

Water awoke to find the other three leaders talking quietly nearby, noticing Root's dark red pelt among their huddle. He hauled himself to his paws and stumbled over. Runt noticed him first, breaking away to come and lend his skinny shoulder. Water accepted gratefully, while Deerface also trotted over to help.

"Wind is the new leader of the exiles. He betrayed Silver," Water croaked, shaking off their help as he regained his balance.

"How would you know such things?" Spatula questioned him tensely.

Water turned his amber gaze on her, and she froze. "In my dream I was visited by Bear, and she explained many things to me, because she is my spirit-rabbit."

"Bear…" Spatula's gaze grew wide and distant. She slowly looked up to meet Water's eyes. "How is she doing?"

"She says that she and Stewie miss you very much, and that Daisy misses Runt terribly. They are watching over us constantly," Water reassured her.

Runt looked down and away, but not before Water caught a glimpse of the pain in his eyes.

"Also," Water continued, "Bear said that she, Stewie, and Daisy have fought off Billy and Eagle many times when they have come to kill me in my sleep. She took me to the exile camp in my dream, where we overheard Billy telling Wind that I was dead, left behind by the rest of you, and that it was Deerface's fault that I had abandoned him."

"Hold on a second, are you saying that Billy is *alive?*" Runt ears pricked in bewilderment. He exchanged baffled glances with the other leaders.

"No, but he killed Wind's spirit-rabbit to take his place. The First Rabbits were blind to this because Slate was stripped of his extra abilities for killing Billy."

"But didn't *Deerface* kill Billy?" Root shook her head as if to clear it.

"No," Deerface hung his head as he admitted. "Slate took over and killed him, since I couldn't do it. It was a terrible mistake, I realize. Billy roams free now, and Slate is helpless, because I didn't kill Billy myself."

"We can fix this," Root insisted, standing taller and looking around in an attempt to inspire optimism in the other rabbits. "Billy will be the helpless one if we can turn Wind against him by showing him that you are alive!"

"Root, Water cannot go anywhere for a while because of the injuries he has suffered, and Wind is too dangerous and unpredictable to bring here," Spatula said quietly, looking down as she softly shook her head. "The goal of the battle was to kill Water, and the only reason that Wind would pay a visit would be to finish the job."

"So, what? We just let rabbits *die* from a war that we could have easily stopped? I'm sorry if none of you can see that casting out Wind was a huge mistake, but I would hope you could see now that continuing to push him away now will also be a huge mistake." Root glared defiantly at the leaders, each at least having the decency to appear to be ashamed. "You were the ones to decide to do this to him, so you are the ones who must fix it. If you don't do something, then I will."

"Root is right. All Wind ever wanted was to be accepted and to be told the complete truth, to have some rabbit, *any* rabbit, trust him and love him. If not for every rabbit in our colony, talk to him for me, and for Wind. You told me that Wind and Water would destroy us all, which must have been a reference to this war. Do not let Billy win again." Water puffed out his chest, sharing a glance with Root. She blinked appreciatively at him for his show of support.

"Well, you two make quite the argument," Runt grunted, stretching as if he couldn't stand being still any longer. "Deerface, what do you think?"

"We need to prepare for war, even if Wind does see that Water is alive. But if Wind is to come here, I want guards posted at every tunnel entrance, and around Wind," Deerface snapped, angry at being overruled.

"No, I want to speak with Wind on the moorland, in the place where we used to meet regularly. He will feel comforted there," Water argued fiercely.

"And how do you expect to get there? Fly?" Deerface shot back.

"I'll *walk* there. Spatula and Root can come with me, as well. Wind hates Deerface, and I'm sure he won't take kindly to Runt, either."

"No way!" Deerface objected, eyes wide with disbelief. "That's the most ridiculous thing I've ever heard. It's suicide!"

Water squared up to him. "I'd rather die trying to make peace than die fighting a pointless war."

"War is the path *toward* peace. It is a *process*, and we must have patience, not just jump into doomed, useless plans. You will *not* go through with this," Deerface growled sharply.

"You cannot stop me."

"Fine, go ahead! I tried to protect you, I *tried* to stop the prophecy, no, the *warning*, from being fulfilled, but I guess I can't stop you from killing us all. Slate told me that I could settle this, but he underestimated your blindness."

Water leaned forward until he and Deerface were nose to nose, and he was staring down into the brown-and-white-furred leader's eyes. "*Slate* is the blind one. He had his powers taken *before* he gave you that prophecy. Have you considered that he wanted to stay important, maybe look good in the eyes of the First Rabbits, so as to regain their trust? He does not deserve your loyalty. The rabbits here and now do."

Deerface looked back, his eyes flashing as if his mind was racing, dashing desperately from one solution to the next.

He is flawed in the way that he must always have some plan, something to tell him what happens next, and that is why he relies too heavily on Slate.

"Slate is wise, and he cares about all of us, *including* Wind."

Water straightened up. "You've expected him to be wise enough for the both of you for far too long.

I'm going to go and fix this. As a leader, I believe that being able to ensure a future is much more important than being able to predict one."

When Deerface was silent, Water signaled to Spatula and Root, heading for the tunnel that lead directly to the moorland.

"Do you really think Slate made up the prophecy?" Spatula asked worriedly as they finally exited the dark tunnels, emerging out onto the sweep of grassy hills, the trees a dark smudge far in the distance.

"I think he was lucky enough to guess one thing: this island does need some cleansing," Root muttered, her brown eyes scanning the route at their paws.

Water twitched his ears in silent agreement. "Come on, let's get this over with."

CHAPTER TWENTY-TWO

A fat raindrop splashed onto Wind's nose, and he sneezed, jumping to his paws and glancing up in disgust. A thick, menacing cluster of dark gray clouds had rolled in, chasing out what light the trees had never managed to completely blot out.

All around him, exiles made quickly for cover as the air turned heavy with moisture, ducking into shallow ditches under logs and small alcoves in the walls of the camp. Wind snorted, settling back down and resting his head on the muddy earth between his front paws, flattening his ears to his back as the rain pelted down. He narrowed his eyes after several moments, considering retreating to his dry, secluded den behind the split boulder.

"You'll catch your death out here."

Wind glanced up to see Jo, looking thin beneath her drenched fur. Her eyes were guarded, cold. Since his first day in the camp, with its cruel way of living that he had been forced to adapt to, he knew that Jo too had been hardened, changing from the softer, gentler and loving rabbit she had once been. Billy had protected her from becoming like an exile, but Billy was dead. She had soon found that a kit was a burden, and that she must put herself first in order to survive.

"What's it to you? If Darkside likes being pestered as much as he pesters me, then I'm sure he'll be more fond of your company."

"I heard about Water."

"You can hear just about anything if you wander in your own mind for long enough."

"May I finish?" Jo stood her ground.

"I have all the time in the world, so you may as well humor me," Wind growled sarcastically.

She sat down slowly, nursing an apparent pain in her side. *She's growing old.*

"I hate seeing all of my kits killing one another. It's an endless cycle: Runt killed Claw, so Billy tries to kill Runt, but ends us being killed by his own kit, so now the exiles killed Water, and feel that that is not enough. Well, I'm saying to you now that this is *enough*. Please, Wind, make peace with the colony. We are all too much alike to *do* this to one another. Some rabbit has to take a stand."

Wind snarled as he arose. "If you ever loved Billy, then you should fight alongside me. He told me to avenge him, told me to avenge Water, and so I *will* stop this. I will kill every single rabbit who ever wronged him, starting with the Three, because they took advantage of him from the very start. I will cleanse this island of them, and then you may enjoy your *peace*," he spat, stalking off to his den.

Before he reached it, Wind felt a searing blow to his haunches, and spun around, poised to fight. Billy glared at him, unrelenting.

"What was that for?" Wind concentrated on controlling his rising anger.

"For talking to my mate like that. She is your mother." Billy didn't *appear* furious.

"I told her what you wanted, all right? Did I leave something out?"

"No, it's *how* you told her. She is not the enemy, and words will not avenge us."

"I know, but I haven't the time to just throw out my plans on a whim and suddenly forget everything the colony has taken from us. She never cared for Water like I did, seeing that she never even saw him after she was exiled. She couldn't *possibly* understand."

"Jo has never had to fight a war, never had to kill." Billy examined his claws nonchalantly. "She was exiled for loving me."

"I have to go, or else I'll never get all of this rain out of my fur." Wind excused himself, now hurrying toward the safety and comfort of his den as the storm continued outside.

CHAPTER TWENTY-THREE

Water stopped, panting in the shade of the overhanging rock. He could almost imagine his own scent mingling with Wind's as they talked quietly, two wronged brothers seeking comfort amidst their own misery. He blinked, and the illusion was gone.

Root flicked mud off her paws and shook out her fur. "The rain yesterday certainly didn't make getting here any easier," she commented wryly.

"It needs to be done," Water grunted, allowing Spatula to check his wounds once more.

"The cuts are getting better. But I'm surprised the trek here didn't cause them to reopen. I'm sure that meeting Wind will at least help to heal the wounds between our two groups, as well."

"If you'd lend me some of your confidence, that'd be great," Root huffed.

"I would if that were possible. Now, should I go to find an exile to fetch Wind for us?" Spatula asked.

"It's better if I do it myself. Alone." Water hoisted himself up again.

"Are you sure?" both Root and Spatula asked in unison.

"I don't want Wind to think that he's walking into an ambush. I'll bring him here, where we can talk—in private."

Water turned and limped painstakingly down the shallow hill, crushing down his nervousness. He scanned the tree line with his eyes, approaching slowly. "Hello?" he called out. "If any rabbit is there and listening, I'd like to speak to my brother, Wind."

Water heard a shuffle of leaves, followed by a loud snap, and then silence. With a sigh, he sat down right on the border, waiting. He waited a long while, continuously glancing up at the sun, watching it set.

Finally, the bushes in front of him shook, parted, and Wind walked through, hostility in his eyes, his stance confident and powerful. He drew up short when he caught sight of Water, and the bravado seemed to drain right out of him.

"I-I thought you were dead!" Wind started toward him, but then stopped, shaking his head roughly. "But Billy told me—"

"Our father lied to you. I almost died, but I recovered, and was then warned of his deception. Once I learned what he had done, and what he had put you through, I knew I had to risk coming to show you the truth. He is not your spirit-rabbit, Wind. The only power he has is manipulation, and it's proving to be very effective. But the truth he's worked so hard to hide from you is that we can stop this war, make peace between our two colonies. You and I can do that."

"You called the exiles a colony." Wind breathed. Then his eyes widened, staring at something just over Water's shoulder. "Look out!"

CHAPTER TWENTY-FOUR

Wind paused, gathering his thoughts. *Water is alive. Billy lied to me. They want to make peace. Well, so do I.*

He looked up, jaws parted to deliver his reply, when he caught sight of a gray-and-white shadow creeping up just behind his oblivious littermate.

Billy! Their eyes met for a split second, his father's glittering with malice. *No! He's going to kill Water!*

Billy finally sprang, but Wind was faster, bowling Water over, both hitting the ground forcefully. Billy missed, skidding away. Water screeched, and Wind scrambled off of him, noticing the wound in his brother's side had opened, the blood pooling rapidly.

"Water? Water, no! Say something, please! I didn't mean to hurt you. Billy was behind you, and—"

He was cut off as thundering pawsteps descended the hill, followed by the shout, "What have you *done*?" He recognized Spatula seconds before she snarled at him, standing between him and Water, before turning and tending quickly to him.

"Where's Root?" Water murmured.

"She went to get help. Deerface was right. This was suicide." Spatula sounded sorrowful.

"No," Water cried weakly in protest.

"Hey, take it easy, all right? I know you wanted for there to be peace, but it was out of our control. Focus on healing up."

"Spatula, I didn't mean to—" Wind began.

"Get away from here, Wind. You have done more than enough. I hope you're happy. Doing this—this coldhearted thing? You aren't even a rabbit at all, so leave. Never return." She snatched up a large leaf from a nearby plant and gently applied it to Water's injury. By now, his brother was completely unconscious. "He could barely even walk here, and you just..." Spatula trailed off, glancing up as Root arrived with Deerface, Chill, Runt, Light, and Mud.

Deerface, Light, and Chill pelted toward him, and Wind took one last horrified and regretful glance at Water before sprinting away, making for the woods. He crashed through the underbrush and heard his pursuers halt.

"Let him go, he'll soon get what he deserves!" Deerface ordered loudly.

Wind eventually had to slow down to a stop, gasping for breath.

No, I didn't kill Water. This is Billy's fault.

EPILOGUE

"Billy, have you anything to say in your defense?"

"I don't answer to you."

"Very well."

Five powerful, majestic rabbits were lined up in a row, looking down from their smooth stone perch, eyes alight with fathomless wisdom and understanding. Around them spread endless, beautiful moorland, crossed by snaking, bubbling streams and even a waterfall. Heather blossoms bloomed and thrived under the generous warmth of the sun—the most perfect place.

One of the rabbits, a female with a superior gray gaze, gestured toward the landscape, her eyes quizzical. "You have been granted a place that you never deserved in this land, and yet, you wished to walk among our living descendants?"

"Under you, there is no form of order or rank. Rabbits just waste their time, roaming aimlessly, never having a purpose. I can't stand it! I need an enemy to fight, just as I always have."

"We cannot allow you to nurture the habits you had while you lived," another warned solemnly.

A growl resonated from deep in Billy's throat. "I was guiding my son! Is that a crime, wishing to be with my family?"

"You killed *one of your sons. This is not up for debate."*

"I haven't killed any of them. Wind got Water out of the way before I could finish him off."

"Water will be with us shortly. He does not deserve to die, but, credits to you, he lost too much blood. He was still young, he had a high rank and a loving mate who one day would have birthed his kits. He was a true credit to rabbit-kind, with a pure heart and a clear mind. You not only stole his life from him, you stole it from the ones who loved him."

Billy's anger only steepened. "You cannot do this! Just grant him life once more, they will never know he died, and then I can live in your stinking, boring meadows."

Slate padded toward them from the fields, his eyes dark. "First Rabbits, he would have killed another of his sons, Deerface, had I not intervened. As a spirit-rabbit, it is my purpose, my duty, to do whatever it takes to keep the one I have always protected alive. Have you forgiven me?"

"Slate, you delivered the warning that was interpreted in your visions, but they did not believe you. The prophecy was fulfilled, yes, but it was too late for Water."

"Where is Bear?"

"Still trying to save Water. She is desperate."

Slate bowed his head in grief. "Tell me, how was my prophecy fulfilled?"

One of the First Rabbits sighed. "They cleansed the island of Billy, and he made it so. He shall be sent away to wander forever in the Utter Darkness."

Billy looked horrified. "What? No—I will keep your rules if you spare me another chance." Billy was starting to fade away, bewilderment the last expression on his scarred face before he was gone completely.

"Slate, you have been forgiven." The First Rabbits gazed seriously down at the black-furred spirit-rabbit.

"We want you to show us what will become of our descendants after Water joins us."

"Of course." Slate closed his eyes, and images flashed in his mind's eye.

"What do you see?"

"A litter of kits, in the exile camp. They are playing. Oh, here comes their father."

"Show us."

"Hey, settle down, now!" a slim, orange-furred female rabbit with green eyes called out.

"I've got this," a battle-scarred, light-gray male told her quietly, nuzzling her affectionately with a muzzle that was laced with distinct scars, before padding toward his kits.

They all turned. Glancing at one another and whispering excitedly, all five kits suddenly pelted at their father, squeaking happily. They tackled him, and he fell over dramatically, pretending to be beaten.

"We got you! Now you have to show us the moorland!"

"Yeah, we wanna see the sunlight, not the trees!"

His face turned serious. "Maybe one day, but we aren't on good terms with the moorland colony right now." His blue eyes darkened with sadness.

"When will we be on good terms?" a female kit asked earnestly, her brown eyes wide.

"I can't really say."

They looked crestfallen, their playful mood gone in an instant.

"Maybe you can let them see the moorland from the tree line?" their mother suggested from where she lay, stretched out in a patch of sunlight.

The gray rabbit looked troubled. "I can't put them in any danger. If the moorland colony even catches a trace of my scent, they'll track me down and kill me, and then the rest of you."

"We moved our camp, Wind. There's no way they could track you over the stream, past the marshes, and then past that clearing where the onions grow. Our colony is *safe* here," she reasoned.

He sighed. "Safety doesn't exist in the world we brought our kits into, not anymore. Now that I have a family, I cannot take the risks I used to. Not only ours, but many kits have been born into our new colony. I must do my duty to protect them all. After all, this is war."

Made in the USA
Monee, IL
05 April 2021

63817266R00108